# FaithWeaver™
# Children's
# Messages 2

Loveland, Colorado

**FaithWeaver™ Children's Messages 2**
Copyright © 2000 Group Publishing, Inc.

**Credits**
Contributing Authors: Jacqui Baker, Tim Baker, Mikal Keefer, Jan Kershner, Kelly Martin, Julie Meiklejohn, Siv M. Ricketts, and Amy Simpson
Editor: Debbie Gowensmith
In-House Editor: Linda A. Anderson
Quality Control Editor: Jan Kershner
Chief Creative Officer: Joani Schultz
Copy Editor: Stephen Beal
Art Director: Anita M. Cook
Cover Art Director: Jeff A. Storm
Cover Designer: Lisa Chandler
Computer Graphic Artist: Shelly Dillon
Cover Photographer: Bohm/Marrazzo
Illustrator: Jan Knudson
Production Manager: Peggy Naylor

ISBN 0-7644-2222-7

10 9 8 7 6 5 4 3 2 1  09 08 07 06 05 04 03 02 01 00
Printed in the United States of America.

# Contents

# Introduction

**W**elcome to the second book in the *FaithWeaver™ Children's Messages* series! These are not your everyday, ordinary children's messages. Instead of having children sit and passively listen to what amounts to an abbreviated version of an adult sermon, these messages engage kids, surprise them, and draw them into spiritual growth. Your children will not only have fun, but will walk away with a deeper understanding of how Bible stories apply to their lives.

Each message in *FaithWeaver Children's Messages 2* explores one Bible story, helping children to experience what happened to the people in the story. These experiences lead children to understand a Bible verse that contains a core biblical truth. For example, children will wrap themselves in towels as "caterpillars" and emerge as "butterflies" to learn, as Saul did on the road to Damascus, that people who believe in Jesus are new creations. This kind of active learning makes sense to children and therefore cements biblical truths in their hearts.

All of your children will look forward to hearing the children's message every week. The messages appeal to children from preschool age through elementary school age. Be sure to attend to the special needs of younger students during your children's message time, and encourage older students to help younger ones with the activities. You can also involve your congregation members, who will be refreshed by new perspectives from these messages—and from the children! You may use a microphone or repeat what children say, hold up props so congregation members can experience the stories as kids do, and even encourage your congregation to cheer or sing along with the kids. These Bible-based children's messages will touch both children's and adults' lives.

We've arranged *FaithWeaver Children's Messages 2* to parallel the four quarters (fall, winter, spring, summer) that most churches use for Sunday school and other educational programs. The book contains four sections of thirteen sermons—one sermon a week for an entire year. The fall quarter begins with the Israelites crossing the Red Sea and follows them as they travel to the Promised Land. For the winter and spring quarters, we cover the New Testament stories of Jesus' birth, life, death, and resurrection so children can focus on Christ during Christmas and Easter. Then the summer quarter returns to the Old Testament and the adventures of Bible heroes such as Gideon, Ruth, and David.

Use the messages in the order suggested here, rearrange them to coincide with holidays or events, or choose Bible stories and verses that fit your own themes. The Bible stories listed in the table of contents and the Scripture index will help you choose the Bible stories and Scriptures you want to teach.

You can also use this book in conjunction with Group's FaithWeaver™ curriculum for Fall 2000 through Summer 2001, which you can order from your local Christian bookstore. Using *FaithWeaver Children's Messages 2* along with this family ministry curriculum helps you reinforce Bible stories and verses in a way that cements Bible truths in kids' lives.

SECTION
# ONE

# FALL
## QUARTER

# The Israelites Cross the Red Sea

## Bible Story: Exodus 13:17–14:31

> **Bible Verse:** "He restores my soul. He guides me in paths of righteousness for his name's sake. Even though I walk through the valley of the shadow of death, I will fear no evil, for you are with me; your rod and your staff, they comfort me" (Psalm 23:3-4).

**Simple Supplies:** *You'll need a Bible, a flashlight, two chairs set up back-to-back, one mini-flashlight for each child (optional), and a volunteer.*

Have any of you ever been in a place where it was really dark? What did that feel like? What can help you see when it's really dark? *Pause for responses.* When we're having lots of troubles, we sometimes say we're going through a dark time. Today we're going to talk about a dark time for God's people, the Israelites.

God's people had been slaves in Egypt for a long time, but God made it possible for them to escape. And although the Israelites were very happy about that, they went from being slaves to being wanderers in the desert. They didn't know where they were or where they were going. It was almost like being in the dark, and they were afraid. Have you ever felt this way? Tell me about it. *Pause for children to respond. Then have the children gather closely around you—especially younger children who may be afraid of the dark. Have a volunteer turn out the lights. Turn on your flashlight, and point it toward the ceiling.*

Even through the dark, difficult times, God always was with the Israelites. The Bible tells us that God "went ahead of them in a pillar of cloud to guide them on their way and by night in a pillar of fire to give them light." God always was right there, guiding the Israelites through their dark times. Let's see what it might have been like to follow God's pillar of fire through darkness.

*Lead kids around the worship area, using the flashlight to guide the way. If possible, lead the children behind, under, and around things. At the end of your "walk," lead kids to the chairs you set up before the message. Have the kids sit down, and have your volunteer turn on the lights again.*

Now Pharaoh was the ruler of all Egypt; Pharaoh is another word for king. As the Israelites followed God through the desert, Pharaoh decided he wanted his slaves back. His army came after the Israelites, who seemed to be trapped because the Red Sea—a very large lake—was all that lay in front of them. *Point out the chairs.* What could God's people do now? They were stuck!

God told Moses to stretch out his staff across the water. *Hold your flashlight over the chairs.* A great wind parted the water and made a dry path through the Red Sea. *Separate the two chairs so kids will be able to walk between them.* God's people walked through the sea on dry land! *Have kids walk between the chairs.* Pharaoh's army tried to cross the sea, too, but the water came back together. *Push the chairs back together, and have kids sit in a circle.*

What do you think it would have been like for the Israelites to follow God through the desert and then through the Red Sea? *Pause for children to respond.* God protected and guided the Israelites during their dark times, and God can protect and guide us during our dark times, too. *Open your Bible to Psalm 23:3-4, and show the page to the children.* Psalm 23:3-4 says: **"He restores my soul. He guides me in paths of right-**  **eousness for his name's sake. Even though I walk through the valley of the shadow of death, I will fear no evil, for you are with me; your rod and your staff, they comfort me."** We never have to be afraid of evil because God is with us. No matter how dark or scary things get, God will guide us just as he guided the Israelites.

Let's thank God for guiding us through our dark times. I'll begin the prayer and then pass around this flashlight. When it comes to you, you can  tell God "Thank you for guiding me." Dear God, thank you so much for being with us and guiding us with your shining light. Thank you, especially, for being near us in our dark times. *Pass around the flashlight to give each child an opportunity to pray. If a child doesn't want to pray aloud, have him or her pray silently, then pass the flashlight to the next child in the circle. Then close the prayer.* God, please help us to remember to trust in you always. In Jesus' name, amen.

*As children return to their seats, give each child a mini-flashlight (if you have them) as a reminder of God's guidance and light.*

# God Sends Quail and Manna

## Bible Story: Exodus 16:1-26

Bible Verse: "You prepare a table before me in the presence of my enemies. You anoint my head with oil; my cup overflows. Surely goodness and love will follow me all the days of my life, and I will dwell in the house of the Lord forever" (Psalm 23:5-6).

**Simple Supplies:** *You'll need a Bible, a large cup, small paper cups, and a large bowl of snacks such as bite-sized crackers. Place the snacks where children can't see them.*

Ask the children to gather around you. Let's take a vote. If you're hungry and would like something to eat, please raise your hand. *Pause for children to respond.* There are quite a few hungry people in here! I wonder if we can find anything to eat. I'll count to ten while you look around this area for something to eat. *Encourage children to search for food while you slowly count to ten.*

*When you've reached "ten," have the children gather around you again.* Did you find any food? *Pause for children to respond.* You know, this is a little bit like what happened to God's people, the Israelites. The Bible says that God brought the Israelites out of slavery in Egypt. But afterward when the Israelites were walking in the desert, they became very hungry and couldn't find anything to eat.

When you're hungry and can't find anything to eat, who takes care of you? *Pause for children to respond.* It sounds like when you're hungry, your parents and other people who care about you feed you. You can trust those people to feed you when you're hungry, can't you? Well, when the Israelites were hungry, they forgot how bad things had been in Egypt. They forgot how good God had been to get them out of Egypt. They forgot to trust God to take care of them. Instead, they whined and complained. In our best whiny and complaining voices, let's say, "We're hungry!" Ready? *Lead children in saying, "We're hungry!"*

Do any of you ever whine and complain? *Pause for children to respond.* At times many of us complain instead of being thankful. Let's take a moment to pray and ask God to forgive us. First, think quietly about a recent time when you complained instead of saying "thank you." *Pause for a few seconds of silence.* Now let's pray. Dear God, thank you for all the good gifts we receive. Help us to respond with thankfulness, and forgive us when we complain. In Jesus' name, amen.

God wanted the Israelites to understand that he would always care for them. So even though they complained, God gave them food to eat—quail, which is like chicken, and manna, which is like bread. *As you speak, bring out the bowl of snacks, the large cup, and the small cups.* Just as God cared for the Israelites, he cares for you. God gives us many good things. Can you name some things God gives us? *As the children name things, use the large cup to scoop snacks from the large bowl and pour the snacks into the small cups. Ask the congregation for ideas, too. Make the snacks overflow the small cups.*

God provides a lot of good things for us—so many things that it's as if they overflow in the same way that the snacks overflowed the cups. *Open your Bible to Psalm 23:5-6, and show the page to the children.* Psalm 23:5-6 says, **"You prepare a table before me in the presence of my enemies. You anoint my head with oil; my cup overflows. Surely goodness and love will follow me all the days of my life, and I will dwell in the house of the Lord forever."** This Scripture reminds us that God loves us and takes care of us. God gives us not only food, but also peace, blessings, goodness, love, and—best of all—life with him in heaven. Isn't our God wonderful? Doesn't he deserve our thanks?

*Distribute a cup of snacks to each child before kids return to their seats.*

# God Provides Water

## Bible Story: Exodus 17:1-7

> **Bible Verse: "The Lord is my shepherd, I shall not be in want. He makes me lie down in green pastures, he leads me beside quiet waters" (Psalm 23:1-2).**

**Simple Supplies:** *You'll need a Bible, a stick or cane, a pitcher of water, and a large bowl. Place the pitcher of water and the large bowl behind the pulpit.*

A re you ready to see some amazing things—things you might have thought were impossible? Good! So am I. That's why I'd like you to help me try to do some amazing things with this normal, everyday cane. Ready?

*Lay the cane on the ground.* First we're all going to try to make the cane float in the air—without touching the cane. Let's all look at the cane and make it float. *Pause for a moment and pretend to concentrate on the cane.* Well, this isn't working out very well. Let's see if we can do something else that's impossible. *Ask the children to help you try to do a number of "impossible" things with the cane: Hide the cane in one hand so nobody can see it, tie the cane in a bow, turn the cane into a circle, and tap the cane against the pulpit and get water to flow out of the pulpit.*

*Once you've tried to do the impossible things, explain the situation to the kids.* You know, it's OK that we couldn't do impossible things like make water come out of the pulpit. If we could do those things, they wouldn't be impossible!

We can't do impossible things, but God can. The Bible tells us about many things God did that nobody else can do. Remember how he parted the Red Sea for the Israelites to cross? Why does God do impossible things like that? *Pause.* As he did when he parted the Red Sea, God does impossible things to take care of his people.

Here's another example. When God led the Israelites out of Egypt, they traveled across a huge desert. The desert was very dry and sandy, and the Israelites couldn't find water. The people and their animals became very thirsty. What would you say if you were very thirsty and couldn't find a drink? *Pause.* You'd complain, right? Well, that's what the Israelites did. They complained, bitterly, and Moses cried out to God, "What am I to do with these people?"

God told Moses to go to a certain rock. *Walk to the pulpit.* God told Moses to hit the rock with the cane. *Gently hit the pulpit with the cane.* Moses did as God said. When Moses hit the rock, water came pouring and splashing out. *Hold up the pitcher of water and the bowl, and pour the water from the pitcher to the bowl.* Because God did something that was impossible for people to do, Moses and the Israelites and all their animals were saved!

God takes good care of us, too. *Open your Bible to Psalm 23:1-2, and show it to the children.* Psalm 23:1-2 says, **"The Lord is my shepherd, I shall not be in want. He makes me lie down in green pastures, he leads me beside quiet waters."** God takes care of us just as he took care of the people who needed water in the desert.

What are some ways that God takes care of you? *Encourage children to share. Help children by asking questions like "God gives us family and friends to care for us, doesn't he? Who are family members and friends that care for you?"*

Let's thank God for taking good care of us. God, thank you for taking care of your people in the desert. Thank you for the words in Psalm 23 that remind us that you take care of us, too. Thank you for the people you put in our lives who love and help us. We love you, God. In Jesus' name, amen.

# God Gives the Ten Commandments (Part 1)

## Bible Story: Exodus 19:16–20:21

> **Bible Verse:** "Love the Lord your God with all your heart and with all your soul and with all your strength. These commandments that I give you today are to be upon your hearts" (Deuteronomy 6:5-6).

**Simple Supplies:** *You'll need a Bible, a picture of a stop sign, a picture of a traffic light with the red light glowing, construction paper hearts with the words "Love God" on them, craft sticks, and tape.*

Today we're going to talk about some of the Ten Commandments that God gave to Moses and the Israelite people. What exactly is a commandment? *Pause for children to respond.* A commandment is like a rule. Let's think about rules for a minute. Let's think of some of the rules you are asked to follow at home and school. *Pause for children to think.* Turn to a partner, and tell each other some of the rules you follow at home. *Pause for a moment while kids share with each other.* Now tell each other some of the rules you follow at school. *Pause for a moment, then invite kids to share a few responses with the whole group.*

Thanks for telling us about those rules. Now let's see if you know what rules these signs stand for. What rule does this sign tell you to follow?

*Hold up the picture of the stop sign, and pause for responses.* This sign says to stop. Why is it important to follow this sign? What can happen if you don't obey this sign? *Pause for responses.* You can get hurt if you don't obey this sign.

*Hold up the picture of the traffic light.* What rule does this sign tell you to follow? Why is it important to follow it? What can happen if you don't obey this sign? *Pause for responses.* You can get hurt if you don't obey this sign.

It's important for everyone to follow the rules we just talked about. Those rules keep us safe. God loves us and wants us to be safe and happy, and God wants us to treat him and each other very well. So a very long time ago when the Israelites were wandering in the desert after escaping slavery in Egypt, God told their leader, Moses, to come to the top of a mountain. Then God gave Moses his rules for living; today we call those rules the Ten Commandments. They tell us how we should treat God and how we should treat other people. How do you think God wants us to treat him? *Pause for children to respond.*

The Ten Commandments teach us to worship only God, to avoid using God's name in a bad way, and to spend the Sabbath day remembering God and all the good things he's done for us.

 In fact, there's another place in the Bible that sort of sums up how we should treat God. *Open your Bible to Deuteronomy 6:5-6, and show kids the passage.* Deuteronomy 6:5-6 says, **"Love the Lord your God with all your heart and with all your soul and with all your strength. These commandments that I give you today are to be upon your hearts."**

How can we love God with all our hearts and souls? *Pause for children to respond.* We can show God we love him with all our hearts and souls by obeying his commandments. Sometimes obeying God takes strength. How can you use your strength to obey God? *Pause for children to respond.* Remember the signs we looked at earlier? If your ball rolled into the street, you might want to run after it even if you saw a red light that told you it wasn't safe to go into the street. It might take all your mind's strength to obey the light, but you'd be safe. In the same way, obeying God's rules helps to keep us safe. Obeying God's rules also shows God that we love him.

The Bible says we should keep God's commandments in our hearts. Let's make heart signs to remind ourselves to follow God's rules. *Give each child a construction paper heart and a craft stick. Set out tape. Show kids how to tape a craft stick to the back of a heart to make a sign.*

*Gather kids in a circle with their signs.* Hold up your hearts as we pray. Dear God, thank you for giving us rules to keep us safe and happy. Help us to love you with all of our hearts, and souls, and strength. And help us to treat you the way you want us to. In Jesus' name, amen.

Take your heart signs home to remind you how to treat God.

---

# God Gives the Ten Commandments (Part 2)

## Bible Story: Exodus 19:16–20:21

> **Bible Verse:** "Jesus replied, ' "Do not murder, do not commit adultery, do not steal, do not give false testimony, honor your father and mother," and "love your neighbor as yourself" ' " (Matthew 19:18b-19).

**Simple Supplies:** *You'll need a Bible.*

Let's talk about what happened when God told the Israelites about the Ten Commandments. First let's think about what life might have been like before God told the people about the commandments. To do this, I'd like you to play a game. *Quickly designate groups of about five children who are sitting close to each other, and have each group sit in a circle.* Our game is called Quick Rhyme, and you can go ahead and play it now for a minute. *Let children try to play the game. If kids say they don't know how, encourage them to keep trying.*

*After about a minute, get the children's attention again.* What was it like to try to play a game without knowing the rules? *Pause for children to respond.* Not knowing the rules can be pretty confusing, can't it? How would trying to play a game without knowing the rules be like living life without knowing how God wants us to live? *Pause for responses.*

God knew that his people needed rules to understand how to treat him and each other the way they should. To help his people, God told them how he wanted them to live; we call God's rules the Ten Commandments.

To think about the difference the Ten Commandments make in our lives, let's play Quick Rhyme again. This time, choose one person to start the game. Start a slap-clap rhythm by slapping your legs twice and then clapping twice. Start slowly so everyone can keep up. Keep up this rhythm throughout the game. When you start, the first person in your group will say a word. On the next claps, the second person in the group must say a word that rhymes with the first person's word. Keep this up until everyone in the group has had a chance to rhyme. The object of the game is for everyone in your group to say a word that rhymes.

*Have kids play the game for a minute.* You did a great job of playing Quick Rhyme. How was playing the game different this time? How does knowing the rules compare to not knowing the rules? What difference do you think knowing God's commandments makes? *Pause for responses.*

Knowing God's rules helps us treat God and others as we should. How do you think God wants us to treat other people? *Pause for responses.* In the Ten Commandments, God says we should honor our mothers and fathers, shouldn't kill anyone, and should love the people we are married to. The commandments say we shouldn't steal, lie, or feel upset when someone gets something we'd like to have.

God knows best how we should treat each other. In fact, these commandments are so important that Jesus talks about them again, much later in the Bible.

*Open your Bible to Matthew 19:18b-19, and show children the passage.* In Matthew 19:18b-19, Jesus repeats what the Ten Commandments tell us. Listen to what Jesus says: " 'Do not murder, do not commit adultery, do not steal, do not give false testimony, honor your father and mother,' and 'love your neighbor as yourself.' "

In this passage, Jesus sums up what the Ten Commandments say about how we should treat each other. When Jesus says we should love our neighbors as ourselves, what does he mean? Who are our neighbors? *Pause for responses.* When Jesus talks about our neighbors, he doesn't mean just the people who live next door. He means everybody we meet every day! Look at all the people in our group. *Pause.* Now look at all the people in this room. *Pause.* Jesus wants us to treat *everyone* the way we'd like to be treated.

Let's thank God for helping us treat each other nicely. *Have kids stand in a circle and hold hands.* I'm going to pray that God will help us treat others in the nice ways we like to be treated. When I finish praying, I'll squeeze the person's hand on my left. That person will squeeze the hand of the person next to him or her. Jesus says we should pass good feelings to each other by loving our neighbors, so that's what we are doing when we pass the squeeze around the circle. Let's pray. Dear God, thank you for teaching us how to get along. Help us to love our neighbors and treat them in the nice ways we like to be treated. *Squeeze the hand of the child to your left. When the squeeze comes back to you, say:* In Jesus' name, amen.

# The Israelites Worship a Golden Calf

## Bible Story: Exodus 32:1-25

> **Bible Verse:** "I am the Lord your God, who brought you out of Egypt, out of the land of slavery. You shall have no other gods before me" (Exodus 20:2-3).

**Simple Supplies:** *You'll need a Bible; a trash can; and several pictures of things people worship such as movie stars and sports figures that children will recognize, cartoon characters, and money.*

Let's talk a little bit about worship today. Everybody knows that we're supposed to worship God. But often we end up worshipping someone or something that isn't God. We are more concerned with those people and those things than we are with God. We put those people and those things before God, as though we are worshipping *them*. Can you tell me some of the different kinds of things that people put before God? *Pause for children to respond, then hold up the pictures you brought.* People put all kinds of things before God—money, toys, other people, food, and so on.

The Bible tells us about a time the Israelites made the mistake of putting something before God. The Israelites' leader, Moses, went up on a mountain to talk with God. Moses was on the mountain for a long time, and the people started to get impatient. In fact, they thought Moses might *never* come back. So they decided to make a brand new god to lead them.

Moses' brother Aaron was sort of like Moses' assistant. So the people went to Aaron and told him, "Make some gods for us who will lead us." Then Aaron told the people to bring all their gold earrings to him. When Aaron had collected all the earrings, he melted them down and then shaped the gold to look like a calf, a baby cow. *Hold up the pictures you brought.*

When the people saw the calf Aaron had made, they decided to have a party to worship it. This made God very angry because people shouldn't worship anything but God. So Moses came down the mountain and became very angry when he saw the people worshipping the calf. Moses took the golden calf and burned it. Then Moses put pieces of gold in water and made the people drink the gold water so they would think about what they had done. What do you think the gold water tasted like when the people drank it? *Pause for children to respond.*

Why was God angry when the people worshipped the golden calf? How did a statue of a calf compare to God? How do the things in these pictures compare to God? *Pause for responses.*

God was angry when the people worshipped the golden calf. *Open your Bible to Exodus 20:2-3, and show the page to the children.* Here's what God said to the people in Exodus 20:2-3: **"I am the Lord your God, who brought you out of Egypt, out of the land of slavery. You shall have no other gods before me."** God is the one we should put first. God is the only one who deserves our worship. Why do you think God deserves our worship? *Pause for children to respond.* God made us, loves us, and always does the right thing. There are so many reasons we should worship only God! Let's show that we put God first by tearing up these pictures of things people put before God. *Pass around the pictures and allow each child to tear off a piece of the picture. Have a trash can handy so children can put the pieces of paper in the trash can.*

We don't want to put anything before God. Let's pray now and ask God to help us remember to worship only him. I'd like you to repeat each line after me. God, sometimes we want to put other things before you. *Prompt kids to repeat after you.* We know we should worship only you. *Prompt kids to repeat after you.* Help us to put you first. In Jesus' name, amen.

# The Israelites Build the Tabernacle

## Bible Story: Exodus 35:4–36:38

Bible Verse: "And whatever you do, whether in word or deed, do it all in the name of the Lord Jesus, giving thanks to God the Father through him" (Colossians 3:17).

**Simple Supplies:** *You'll need a Bible and, for each child, a box. Boxes can be different sizes and shapes.*

As children come forward, give each one a box. Today we're going to talk about giving to God. To begin, I'd like you to think about some of your things. What are some of your very favorite things? *Pause for children to respond.* Those are really great things, aren't they? Now I want to tell you what God's people, the Israelites, once did with some of their best, most favorite things.

A tabernacle is like a church building, and the Israelites needed to build a tabernacle for God. To do this they needed supplies. Moses, the Israelites' leader, told the people that if they wanted to, they could give what they owned to get the supplies to make the tabernacle. The Israelites brought rings and earrings, cloth and yarn, wood, and more.

Now think about what you would have given to God if you had been with the Israelites. Would you have given the cloth from your clothes? Would you have given your toys? Would you have given your money?

Pretend to put all those things in your box, then bring your box to me. As you set down your box, name the things that you would have given to God. *Pause for children to respond, pointing out where you'd like them to place their boxes.*

Thank you so much for all you've given! You have been as generous as the Israelites when they gave their very best to help build the tabernacle. In fact, they gave so much that Moses had to tell them to stop!

The Israelites didn't just give things, though. Moses asked all the people to contribute their skills and talents to help build the tabernacle. What are some of the skills and talents that you have? *Pause for children to respond.* Each one of you has wonderful skills and talents! The Israelites used their skills and talents to build the tabernacle and all the things that went inside it.

Now let's use our skills and talents to build a "tabernacle."; We'll build the tabernacle with our boxes. As you bring up your box, name a skill or talent that you can use to help God. *Have the children pile their boxes until they've built a pyramid or square. If they need help thinking of abilities, encourage them with suggestions such as singing songs, praying, hugging others, telling others about God, and so on. After kids have piled the boxes, have them sit down around the structure.*

Thank you so much for all you've given! Look at the wonderful tabernacle you've built. You've given to God your very best skills and talents!

I'd like to read a verse to you that tells a little more about what the Israelites did. *Open your Bible to Colossians 3:17, and show the page to the children.* Colossians 3:17 says, **"And whatever you do, whether in word or deed, do it all in the name of the Lord Jesus, giving thanks to God the Father through him."** In all our words and actions, we can show that we love God. The Israelites showed that they loved God by giving their things and their skills and talents to build a tabernacle. With your words, how can you show God your love? With your actions, how can you show God your love? *Pause for children to respond.* We can show our love for God by saying kind words to God and to each other, by giving to others, and by doing what God wants us to do.

Let's say the Bible verse and do some hand motions. *Have children repeat the following words and motions after you a few times.* "And whatever you do..." *Hold out your hands.* "...whether in word..." *Point to your mouth with both index fingers.* "...or deed..." *Clasp your hands together in front of you.* "...do it all..." *Spread out your arms in front of you.* "...in the name of the Lord Jesus..." *Point to heaven.* "...giving thanks..." *Shake your hands above your head.* "...to God the Father through him." *Point to heaven.*

Great job! We don't have to build a big tabernacle for God for him to be happy. We can show God that we love him in everything we say and do.

Now let's pray and ask God to help us do great things for him. As you take a box from the tabernacle we've built, pray, "Dear God, help me to do wonderful things for you. In Jesus' name, amen." Then you can take your box home to help you remember to give your very best to God. *Help children remove the boxes and repeat the prayer.*

# Moses Sends Spies Into the Promised Land

## Bible Story: Numbers 13:1–14:23

Bible Verse: "Therefore, my dear brothers, stand firm. Let nothing move you. Always give yourselves fully to the work of the Lord, because you know that your labor in the Lord is not in vain" (1 Corinthians 15:58).

**Simple Supplies:** *You'll need a Bible; three to six volunteers to play spies; funny sunglasses, hats, bandannas, or similar spy disguises; scissors; and the "Spies' Report" handout (p. 23). Before the message, photocopy the handout and cut out the cards. To each volunteer "spy," give a card and a disguise. If you have fewer than six volunteers, just be sure all the spy reports are read. Ask the volunteers to sit toward the front, put on the disguises at the beginning of the children's message, and read from their cards when it's time.*

Hi, everyone. I want to play a pretending game with you today. First, can you tell me who Moses was? *Pause for children to respond.* God helped Moses lead the Israelites out of slavery in Egypt. Let's pretend that I'm Moses, and you can pretend to be the Israelites. Ready? Here we go!

*Point into the distance.* Wow, look at that land over there! God has promised to give us that land. It looks like a *great* place to live! *Lead the children in cupping their hands around their eyes as "binoculars" to pretend to look to a distant place.* I've sent spies to that land to find out more about it for us. Can you help me find the spies? They're seated with our people. *Encourage the children to walk around the congregation and look for the spies. Have children bring the spies to the front as they find them. If they have trouble finding the spies, give children hints as to what disguises the spies are wearing.*

Now let's all sit and listen to what the spies learned about the land God promised to give us. *Have the volunteers read the cards in order. Afterward, thank the volunteers and have them return to their seats.*

Our spies found out some interesting things. What are some reasons we shouldn't live in that land? *Pause for children to respond.* But what about the spies who say God will help us? What do you think about that? *Pause.*

You did a great job of pretending today. What happened during our game is a lot like what happened with the Israelites in the Bible. God promised to help the Israelites and to give them the land, but most of the spies convinced the Israelites that they shouldn't trust God. Only two spies stood up for God. They told the people that the land would be a very good place to live and that God would be with them. Those two spies stood firm, knowing that the Israelites could trust God.

*Open your Bible to 1 Corinthians 15:58, and show the page to the children.* First Corinthians 15:58 says, **"Therefore, my dear brothers, stand firm. Let nothing move you. Always give yourselves fully to the work of the Lord, because you know that your labor in the**

**Lord is not in vain."** We should always do what God wants us to do, no matter what. Two of the Israelite spies stood firm, trusting God even though no one else did.

Think about a time someone asked you to do something difficult and you did it even though you were scared or overwhelmed. Do you remember times like that? *Allow several children to share their experiences.* See—you've been able to do some really difficult things! And didn't you feel good, knowing that you had tried your best? That's what it's like when we stand firm for God.

Let's pray and ask God to help us stand firm and do what he wants us to do. Dear God, thank you for promising to be with us always. Help us to remember your promise when we need to do difficult things. Help us to stand firm and always do what you want us to do. In Jesus' name, amen.

# Spies' Report

## Spy 1:

The land was very, very good. But we shouldn't try to live there. The people who already live there are too strong for us. They could easily hurt us.

## Spy 2:

A lot of really good fruit grows in the land. We even brought back some grapes and other fruits to show you. But it's no use. The people who live there are so big and powerful. They're like giants! We should just turn around because there's no way we would win if we had to fight against those giants.

## Spy 3:

I've never seen such a beautiful land. If we were able to live there, we'd have huge gardens and plenty of water. But I don't even think we should try to live there. The people live in large cities that are surrounded by walls. How do you fight against that? I give up.

## Spy 4:

I don't know why you are all so afraid. Are you forgetting that God promised this land to us? We should go and take it. I know we can do it— with God's help!

## Spy 5:

You're wrong! We can't take the land because the people are too big and strong. We're like little tiny grasshoppers to them! You know, maybe that land isn't so great after all. Maybe we should just go back to Egypt.

## Spy 6:

No, we shouldn't go back to Egypt. God has always been with us. And God will be with us now. We should live in the land God promised us.

# Balaam's Donkey Talks

### Bible Story: Numbers 22:1-38

> **Bible Verse:** "Come and see what God has done, how awesome his works in man's behalf!" (Psalm 66:5).

**Simple Supplies:** *You'll need a Bible and a puppet. If you don't have a puppet, just glue some buttons, ribbons, and scrap fabric to a sock or paper sack. Or use markers to draw features and clothing on a sock or sack.*

Have any of you ever heard a donkey speak in our language? *Pause for the children to respond.* Have any of you ever heard *any* animal speak in our language? *Pause.* Well, I haven't either, so imagine my surprise when I read in my Bible about a donkey that talked! The man who owned the donkey was named Balaam. *Hold up the puppet.* This is Balaam, and we're going to find out what happened between Balaam and his donkey. But first we have to find out about the message Balaam got from the king.

One day, some men visited Balaam with a message from the king. The king asked Balaam to put a curse on God's people, the Israelites. Balaam had a choice to make. *Point Balaam to your right.* Balaam could choose to curse the Israelites, or *(point Balaam to your left)* Balaam could choose to tell the king "no."

What do you do when you have a hard choice to make? *Pause for responses, then bow Balaam's head.* Balaam talked to God about his tough choice. He asked God what he should do. God told him, "Do not curse the Israelites; they are my people."

Balaam made a choice. *Point Balaam to the left.* The next day, Balaam told the king's messengers that he wouldn't curse the Israelites.

But the king didn't like Balaam's answer. He sent even more messengers to visit Balaam. They said, "The king will make you rich if you come with us and curse the Israelites." Balaam had another choice to make. *Point Balaam to the right.* He could curse the Israelites *(point Balaam to the left),* or he could obey God. *Bow Balaam's head.* Balaam prayed to God again. That night, God told Balaam to go with the messengers but to do only what God told him to do.

The next day, Balaam went with the messengers, riding on his donkey. God wanted to make sure Balaam understood not to curse the Israelites, so he sent an angel to get Balaam's attention. *Move Balaam to the right as if he's riding a donkey.* You all can play the role of the angel. Without making a sound, try to get Balaam's attention. *Encourage the children to wave their hands, point at Balaam, and so on. Continue moving Balaam to the right.*

Balaam's donkey saw the angel and walked off the road. But Balaam didn't see the angel. Do you know what he did? He beat the poor donkey and made it get back on the road.

Once again, the angel stood in the road to get Balaam's attention. *Encourage the children to continue trying to silently get Balaam's attention.*

Balaam still didn't see the angel but the donkey did. This time, the donkey tried to walk around the angel. But Balaam didn't like the donkey not walking straight so he beat the donkey again.

For a third time the angel stood in the road to get Balaam's attention. *Encourage the children to continue trying to silently get Balaam's attention.* This time Balaam's donkey just lay down—right there in the road with Balaam on its back! Balaam was so angry that he beat the donkey with a stick.

How had God tried to get Balaam's attention? *Pause for children to respond.* God does amazing things to get our attention, doesn't he? Then God did another amazing thing. God made the donkey speak to Balaam. The donkey said, "What have I done to you to make you beat me? Haven't I always been good to you? Have I ever given you this trouble before?"

Well, hearing that donkey speak sure got Balaam to pay attention to what was going on. In fact, Balaam finally saw the angel and bowed. Balaam understood that God was with him. He understood that he should not curse God. *Turn the puppet so its face is facing the floor.* God certainly did amazing things to get Balaam's attention. *Set aside the puppet.*

Isn't that an amazing story? *Open your Bible to Psalm 66:5, and show the page to the children.* Psalm 66:5 says, **"Come and see what God has done, how awesome his works in man's behalf!"** God did amazing things for Balaam, and God does amazing things for us, too. How do you think Balaam felt when his donkey started talking? How do you think he felt when he finally saw the angel? *Pause for children to respond.* God is really awesome and does amazing things to help us— even if it takes things like a talking donkey to get our attention.

Let's pray. Thank you, God, for loving us and for doing awesome things to help us. Help us to pay attention to you. In Jesus' name, amen.

# Joshua Becomes Leader of Israel

## Bible Story: Joshua 1:1-11

> **Bible Verse:** "Have I not commanded you? Be strong and courageous. Do not be terrified; do not be discouraged, for the Lord your God will be with you wherever you go" (Joshua 1:9).

**Simple Supplies:** *You'll need a Bible and an adult volunteer.*

*ather children in a large group, then ask them to follow you as you walk around the congregation.* Who are some leaders you know of? What qualities do you think they have that makes them leaders? Have you ever been a leader? When? *Encourage children to answer these questions as you walk. Return to the front by the last answer to the last question.*

All right now. Close your eyes. Imagine I've been your leader for forty years. We've lived together, eaten together, worked together, prayed together, laughed together, and cried together. *Pause for children to consider this idea.* Open your eyes. What kind of relationship do you think we have? Why? *Pause for children to respond.*

Now imagine that after forty years, I'm out of the picture and (volunteer's name) is your new leader. How do you think you'd feel about having a new leader after such a long time? *Pause for responses, then ask the volunteer to lead the group around the congregation. Don't accompany the group. Ask the volunteer to bring the group back after a minute or so. Congratulate the leader on doing a good job and the group for following obediently.*

Moses led the Israelites out of Egypt and around the desert for *forty* years. When Moses died, God made Joshua the leader. With Joshua to lead them, the Israelites were about to enter the land God promised them. I bet the Israelites felt at least a little afraid about their new leader and the big adventure ahead of them.

But God told Joshua and the Israelites to be strong and courageous. *Open your Bible to Joshua 1:9, and show the page to the children.* In Joshua 1:9 God says, **"Have I not commanded you? Be strong and courageous. Do not be terrified; do not be discouraged, for the Lord your God will be with you wherever you go."** God said he would lead Joshua, so Joshua could feel brave in leading the Israelites. God promised that he'd be with Joshua and the Israelites all the time.

I bet some of you will grow up to be leaders in our church and community. Do you think you'll be a better leader by following God or by leading on your own? Why? How can following God help you to be a strong leader? *Pause.*

God promises to always be with us. Let's pray together. We'll be quiet for a bit so you can pray silently for God to give you courage or strength wherever you need it in your life. *Allow fifteen seconds of silence, then lead children in this prayer:* Dear God, give us the strength and courage that come from knowing you are always with us. In Jesus' name, amen.

To close, I want to teach you a rhyme to help you remember what you learned today. *Have children repeat this rhyme after you:* With God by my side and the Bible as my guide, I can be God's leader!

Now march back to your seats and say the rhyme together. Everyone in the congregation can join us. *Repeat the rhyme until the children are at their seats.*

# Joshua Sends Spies to Jericho

## Bible Story: Joshua 2:1-24

> **Bible Verse:** "And without faith it is impossible to please God, because anyone who comes to him must believe that he exists and that he rewards those who earnestly seek him" (Hebrews 11:6).

**Simple Supplies:** *You'll need a Bible.*

I'd like to show you a few signs in sign language. Who uses sign language? Why? *Pause for children to respond.* Let's see if you can guess what this sign means. *Demonstrate the sign for "love." Let kids guess, then tell them it's the sign for "love."* Let's try another sign. *Demonstrate the sign for "God." Let kids guess what it means, then tell them:* OK, let's try one more. *Demonstrate the sign for "Bible." Have kids guess.* This sign means two things. The first part of the sign means "Jesus." *Demonstrate the first part of the sign.* The second part of the sign means "book." *Demonstrate the second part of the sign.* So this sign literally means "Jesus book." What do you think that might be? *Pause.* That's right—the Bible.

Sign language helps people communicate important things with each other. Today we're going to talk about another kind of sign that also communicated something important.

love

God

The Bible tells us that Joshua, who led the Israelites after Moses died, sent two spies to a city called Jericho to see what it was like. Think of a sign you can make with your hands that shows spying. *Let kids show their signs.* The people of Jericho didn't believe in God. But there was one woman in the city who had heard about

Bible

God and believed in God. Her name was Rahab. Rahab wanted to help the spies even though doing so would be very dangerous for her. Think of a sign you can make that shows danger. *Let kids show their signs.*

The king of Jericho came looking for the spies, so Rahab hid them. Think of a sign that shows hiding. *Let kids show their signs.* Then Rahab helped the spies escape and asked them to protect her and her family when all the Israelites came to Jericho. Think of a sign that would ask someone to come back. *Let kids show their signs.* The spies told Rahab to hang a red rope from her window so they would know where she and her family were. They said they would protect her and her family when they came back. Rahab showed faith by helping the spies. Let's read a bit more about what it means to have faith.

*Open your Bible to Hebrews 11:6, and show the page to the children.* Hebrews 11:6 says, **"And without faith it is impossible to please God, because anyone who comes to him must believe that he exists and that he rewards those who earnestly seek him."** We need to believe in God in order to please him. How did Rahab show that she believed in God? Do you think her actions pleased God? *Pause for responses.*

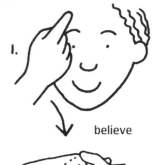

believe

2.

This is the sign for "believe." *Demonstrate the sign.* Rahab showed that she believed in God by helping the spies. How would someone watching the way you live your life know that you believe in God? *Help kids think of ideas such as being kind to others, praying, and talking to other people about God.*

Let's ask God to help us always show signs that we believe in him. Think of a sign that shows you're praying. *Let kids show their signs.* Dear God, thank you for helping us to believe in you. Please help us to show others we believe in you with the signs we show in our lives. In Jesus' name, amen.

*Encourage kids to remember the signs they learned today as reminders of the signs of belief in God they can show in their lives.*

# The Israelites cross the Jordan River

## Bible Story: Joshua 3:1–4:24

Bible Verse: "Give thanks to the Lord, call on his name; make known among the nations what he has done" (1 Chronicles 16:8).

**Simple Supplies:** *You'll need a Bible, stickers, and a sheet or towels.*

The Bible says that the Israelites traveled from slavery in Egypt, through the desert, then finally got to the land God promised them. But when they got to the Promised Land, they realized they had a *big* problem. *Spread the sheet in the middle of the floor. Have the children gather around it.* To get into the Promised Land, they had to cross the Jordan River, which was wide and deep with very fast-moving water. *Show the children how to grip the edge of the sheet and quickly lift it up a few inches and then down in order to make a fast-moving "river."* How do you think the Israelites felt when they saw that big river? What would you have done beside the Jordan River? *Pause for children to respond.*

Joshua said God would do an amazing thing to help them. Has anything amazing happened to you? *Encourage children to share their amazing stories.* What amazing stories! God sure loves us and does amazing things for us!

God did something amazing to help the Israelites, too. When the Israelite priests put their feet in the water, the river stopped flowing. *Step onto the sheet (or have the pastor step onto the sheet), and have children stop moving the sheet. Then gather up the sheet and set it aside.* All the Israelites walked across the river on dry land! How do you think the Israelites felt? *Pause for responses.*

God really did do an amazing thing for the Israelites. If you had been there, what would you have said to God? *Pause for responses.*

*Open your Bible to 1 Chronicles 16:8, and show the page to the children.* In 1 Chronicles 16:8 the Bible says, **"Give thanks to the Lord, call on his name; make known among the nations what he has done."** God does amazing things, and we should thank him and tell others about it. That's just what the Israelites did. They took twelve stones out of the river and built an altar. Everyone who ever saw the stones would know about the amazing thing God had done and would remember to thank God. How can you remember to thank God for the amazing things he's done? *Pause.*

*Distribute stickers.* Every time you see your sticker, think about the amazing things God has done. Then remember to thank God just as the Israelites did when God parted the Jordan River for them to cross. Let's thank God right now for the amazing things he does. Thank you, God, for the amazing things you do. Help us remember to tell others about the amazing things you've done. In Jesus' name, amen.

Let's tell others that God does amazing things. On the count of three, let's all yell, "God does amazing things!" One, two, three: God does amazing things!

# God Gives Victory Over Jericho

## Bible Story: Joshua 6:1-27

Bible Verse: "Humble yourselves, therefore, under God's mighty hand, that he may lift you up in due time. Cast all your anxiety on him because he cares for you" (1 Peter 5:6-7).

**Simple Supplies:** *You'll need a Bible and building blocks.*

**D**ump a pile of building blocks in the center of the group of children. Let's pretend these building blocks are problems people face. Let's think for a moment about those problems. As we name problems people face, we'll build a wall with these blocks. *Hold up a block.* This block can stand for a disagreement you're having with a friend or a sore throat. What other problems can these blocks stand for? *Encourage children to name problems, and have a different child add a block to the wall for each problem. Continue until children run out of ideas or blocks.*

Wow! Look at all these problems! Our problems can build up like this wall until it seems like there's no way we can fix all the problems.

In the Bible, the Israelites faced a big problem that really was a wall. It was a very big wall that surrounded the city of Jericho. The Israelites wanted to enter the city, but the huge wall kept them out. The wall was a big, big problem. But God said he'd help the Israelites. God told the Israelites to march around the city once each day for six days. Let's do as the Israelites did and quietly march around our wall. *Have kids slowly and quietly march around the wall in single file.* On the seventh day, the Israelites marched around the city seven times. The last time around, they shouted, and the wall fell down! They marched right into Jericho!

Let's pretend our wall of problems is the wall around Jericho. Let's knock it down just as God knocked down that wall. *Help kids knock down the wall, making sure no one gets too enthusiastic. Then have the children sit down.* That's what God does with our problems when we trust him. He knocks them down, just as he knocked down the wall around Jericho.

*Open your Bible to 1 Peter 5:6-7, and show the page to the children.*  First Peter 5:6-7 says, **"Humble yourselves, therefore, under God's mighty hand, that he may lift you up in due time. Cast all your anxiety on him because he cares for you."** If we trust God with our problems, he'll take care of us. How can we trust God and give our problems to him? *Pause for responses.*

Now think of one problem you're facing. We're going to do what God asks us to do and give our problems to him. So think silently for a few moments about a problem in your life. *Pause for a few moments while children think.*

Let's pray and give our problems to God. Dear God, thank you for caring about us and for asking us to give our problems to you. Thank you for knocking down the problem walls in our lives. Please take these problems we're thinking of. We trust you to help us. In Jesus' name, amen.

# SECTION
# TWO

# WINTER
## QUARTER

# Prophets Foretell Jesus' Coming

## Bible Story: Jeremiah 33:14-16

> **Bible Verse:** "All this took place to fulfill what the Lord had said through the prophet: 'The virgin will be with child and will give birth to a son, and they will call him Immanuel'—which means, 'God with us' " (Matthew 1:22-23).

**Simple Supplies:** *You'll need a Bible, a skein of colored yarn, and scissors.*

*A*s children gather, ask them to stand in several rows facing the congregation. Give the end of the skein of yarn to the first person in the first row. Ask the child to spin around once or twice so the yarn is wrapped around their arms and middle. Move to the next child and repeat until all the children are wrapped up in the yarn. Children need to still be standing in line close enough that they can whisper to each other.

We're going to play the Telephone game. I'll whisper something to the first person in line, and that person will whisper the phrase to the next person, and so on. We'll ask the last person in line what he or she heard and see how it compares to the message I started off with. *Whisper the phrase "I'm glad you're here today" to the first person in line. Have children pass the message down the first row and the rows behind, and then ask the last child what he or she heard. Play again, beginning with the last child and row and working in the opposite direction. This time use the phrase "Jesus is coming!"*

Now tell me what it's like to be wrapped up in all this yarn. What do you think it would be like to try to live your life wrapped up like this? *Pause for responses.* The Bible tells us that without Jesus, people are trapped in sin just as you're trapped in this yarn. But a long time ago, God gave people an important message. God said he was sending someone to set us free! How would you pass on an important message like that? *Pause.* We pass on news to other people in all kinds of ways. We may talk to people face to face, call them, write them, e-mail them, or even get our message across on the radio or TV or in newspapers or magazines.

Well, God's message was the most important message ever. God wanted the people to know that he was sending Jesus to save them and set them free. Just as we whispered messages in our Telephone game, God whispered messages about Jesus to some very special people; we call those special people prophets. One of those prophets was a man named Jeremiah, who heard God's message and told other people that Jesus was coming. Why do you think God wanted people to know that Jesus was coming? *Pause.* Let's thank God for telling prophets like Jeremiah this wonderful message. Dear God, thank you for telling people that Jesus was coming to save everyone. And most of all, thank you for sending Jesus. In Jesus' name, amen.

*Open your Bible to Matthew 1:22-23, and show the page to the children.* Matthew 1:22-23 says, **"All this took place to fulfill what the Lord had said through the prophet: 'The virgin will be with child and will give birth to a son, and they will call him Immanuel' which means, 'God with us.' "** Before Jesus was born, the prophets knew he'd arrive! Because of God's important message to the prophets, people were waiting for Jesus to arrive.

*Use the scissors to cut the yarn between children. Allow children to un-wrap themselves and hang onto their string.* Jesus was the one God sent to set everyone free from sin. That's an important message to remember and to tell others about, isn't it? Just as the prophets told the people that Jesus was coming, you can tell people that Jesus has come to set everyone free!

*From the yarn kids are holding, cut pieces long enough to tie around kids' fingers. Ask older kids to help you.* People sometimes tie string around their fingers to remind them of things. When you see this piece of yarn on your finger, remember that you can tell others that Jesus came to set us free from sin.

# Zechariah Prophesies About Jesus

## Bible Story: Luke 1:68-79

> **Bible Verse: "For God did not send his Son into the world to condemn the world, but to save the world through him" (John 3:17).**

**Simple Supplies:** *You'll need a Bible and baby pictures of three adults from the congregation.*

L et's begin today by doing some guessing. I have three baby pictures. I want you to look at each picture and tell me about the baby in the picture. I want to know where the baby will live when the baby grows up and what the baby will do. *Show children the pictures, and encourage them to guess. Ask them questions such as "Does this baby look serious or funny? What kind of job might a serious (or funny) person have? Do you think this baby will like the cold weather or the warm weather? So where might this person live?*

Let's see how well we guessed. You described this baby as (summarize the predictions). The baby is here today—it's (name the adult). Please stand up and tell us how accurate our predictions were. *Continue with the other pictures.*

I don't think we'd better get a job predicting the future! But did you know that the Bible tells us about a man who predicted exactly what a baby would do when the baby grew up? Here's the story.

A man named Zechariah had a baby named John. God told Zechariah that when the baby John grew up, he was going to prepare people to meet a very, very special person God was sending to save people from their sins. That's exactly what John grew up to do. Zechariah told people that God would send a baby even more special than John and that this baby would grow up to save the people from their sins. Can you guess who Zechariah was talking about? *Pause for children to respond.* He was talking about Jesus.

Why do you think God told Zechariah about what John and Jesus would do when they grew up? *Pause for responses.* God wanted people to understand who Jesus was. The Bible tells us why this message was so important. *Open your Bible to John 3:17, and show the page to the*  *children.* John 3:17 says, **"For God did not send his Son into the world to condemn the world, but to save the world through him."** God wanted people to know that Jesus was coming to save them from their sins. God sent Jesus to save you, too. When you do wrong things, you can ask God to forgive you and he will! You can also live forever in heaven with God. All you have to do is thank God for sending Jesus to save us and let Jesus be in charge of your life.

Now let's thank God for sending Jesus to save us. And if you want to know more about how Jesus can save you, talk with your mom or dad or come to see me. I like telling people about Jesus!

 Please pray with me. Dear God, thank you for telling Zechariah the wonderful things Jesus would grow up to do. And especially, thank you for sending Jesus to our world to save us. In Jesus' name, amen.

# John Prepares People for Jesus' Coming

## Bible Story: Luke 3:7–18

> Bible Verse: "If we confess our sins, he is faithful and just and will forgive us our sins and purify us from all unrighteousness" (1 John 1:9).

**Simple Supplies:** *You'll need a Bible, a sheet of white paper, a black marker, a pale yellow crayon, and a red transparent folder. Before the sermon, use the yellow crayon to draw a big heart on the white paper. Use the marker to draw an identical heart on the red folder.*

Before we talk about the Bible story, I have a question to ask. Has anyone here ever done anything wrong? If you have, raise your hand. *Raise your own hand, and pause as kids raise their hands. If any children don't raise their hands, don't call attention to the fact. Address the congregation.* How about all of you? If you've ever done anything wrong, please raise your hands. *Pause as kids observe how many people raise their hands.*

It looks as though *everyone* has done wrong things, doesn't it? And that's very true. We all do wrong things. When we do wrong things, that's called sinning. In our Bible story for today, a man named John told people to stop doing wrong things. He told them to clean their hearts to get ready for Jesus.

How do you feel when you've done something wrong? *Pause for kids to respond.* It feels yucky when we do wrong things, doesn't it? What makes you feel better after you've done something wrong? *Pause.* Our Bible verse today tells us what to do when we sin. Listen to what the Bible says in 1 John 1:9. *Open your Bible to the verse, and show the page to the kids.* **"If we confess our sins, he is faithful and just and will forgive us our sins and purify us from all unrighteousness."**

The Bible says that if we tell Jesus what we did wrong and that we're sorry, he'll forgive us and make our hearts clean again. Our sins will disappear from view. I'll show you what I mean.

*Show kids the white paper with the yellow heart on it.* When we do wrong things, our hearts can become all cluttered with sin. *Let each child use the yellow crayon to draw an X inside the heart.* But when we ask Jesus to forgive us, he does. And those sins all disappear. *Place the red folder on top of the white paper, and show the children. The yellow heart with the X's will disappear beneath the red heart.* Jesus forgives us, and our sins disappear. *Set the papers out of view.*

Let's ask Jesus to forgive our sins and make our hearts clean. *Ask everyone, including the congregation, to bow their heads.* Dear Lord, we're sorry for the wrong things we've done. Please forgive us, and make our hearts clean. Thank you for loving us and forgiving us. In Jesus' name, amen.

# The Son of God Is Born!

## Bible Story: Luke 1:26-45; 2:1-20

**Bible Verse: "For to us a child is born, to us a son is given, and the government will be on his shoulders. And he will be called Wonderful Counselor, Mighty God, Everlasting Father, Prince of Peace" (Isaiah 9:6).**

**Simple Supplies:** *You'll need a Bible.*

I want to tell you today about some exciting news that God gave to a woman named Mary. God sent an angel to Mary to tell her she was going to have a baby! The angel said that the baby would be God's Son and would be greater than a king. What do you think it would be like to get that kind of news from an angel? When have you been told exciting news? Why do you think it's great news that God's Son came to earth? *Pause for responses.*

When Mary first heard that she was going to be Jesus' mother, she didn't understand how that could happen. It seemed impossible. But Mary decided that she would trust God. How would you respond if God told you he was going to make a big change in your life? *Pause for responses.*

Nothing is impossible for God. He even sent his Son to become a human baby in order to save people from their sins. Jesus is a great gift to all of us. *Open your Bible to Isaiah 9:6, and show the page to the children.* Isaiah 9:6 says, **"For to us a child is born, to us a son is given, and the government will be on his shoulders. And he will be called Wonderful Counselor, Mighty God, Everlasting Father, Prince of Peace."** Let's thank God. Dear God, nothing is impossible with you. Thank you for the gift of your Son. In Jesus' name, amen.

The verse we read calls Jesus four names. What does a counselor do? Why do you think Jesus is called a Wonderful Counselor? *Pause for responses.* What does it mean to be mighty? Why do you think Jesus is called a Mighty God? *Pause for responses.* What does it mean to be everlasting? What makes Jesus a good Father? *Pause for responses.* When do you feel peaceful? Why do you think Jesus is called the Prince of Peace? *Pause for responses.*

*Have children form four groups, and assign to each group one of the names. Help children create a body posture to represent the names. For example, the Wonderful Counselor group could put their hands behind their ears, the Mighty God group could show arm muscles, the Everlasting Father group could pretend to hold a baby, and the Prince of Peace group could pretend to lay their heads on their hands and sleep. Say the four names and point to the appropriate groups so they can practice their postures.*

I'm going to read Isaiah 9:6 again. When I point to your group, say the name of Jesus that your group represents while doing your body posture. *Review the names of Jesus, then reread the verse.*

Just as an angel told Mary about the birth of Jesus, you've just told the people here that Jesus was born to save us. It's a very important message! Every time you see a baby this week, remember to thank God for sending Jesus.

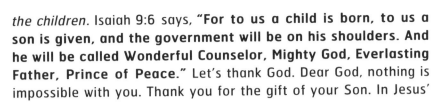

# Jesus Grows Up

## Bible Story: Luke 2:39-52

**Bible Verse: "I and the Father are one" (John 10:30).**

**Simple Supplies:** *You'll need a Bible.*

oday we're going to learn about a time Jesus' family didn't know where he was. You see, every year Jesus went with his family and a group of neighbors to the city of Jerusalem to celebrate a special holiday that honored God. When Jesus was twelve years old, his family went to Jerusalem as usual. Have you ever traveled with your family? Where did you go? What was it like? *Allow a few children to share their stories.*

When the holiday was over, Jesus' parents went back home with the group. They thought Jesus was with the group, but he wasn't. How do you think Jesus' parents felt when they couldn't find him? *Pause for responses.*

Jesus' parents went back to Jerusalem. They found Jesus at the Temple, where people went to worship God. Jesus was talking with the teachers in the Temple, and everyone was amazed at how much Jesus knew about God. When his parents found him, he told them why he was in the Temple. He said, "Didn't you know I'd be here in my Father's house?" Jesus called the Temple his Father's house because people went to the Temple to meet with God. But Jesus was also saying that God was his Father. Why do you think Jesus was in the Temple talking to the teachers? *Pause.*

Think for a moment about what you want to be when you grow up. Who wants to act out what you want to be? *Allow several children to act out what they want to be, and have the rest of the group guess.* Let's talk about what these kids need to do to get ready for the jobs they want. *Encourage other kids to call out ideas of what the kids should do to prepare for their jobs.*

Jesus knew exactly what he was going to be when he grew up; he was going to show all people how much God loves us. So when Jesus was twelve, he wanted to spend lots of time with God and learning about God. The best way to prepare for his future was to spend time in God's house, learning from the teachers.

*Open your Bible to John 10:30, and show the page to the children.* In John 10:30, Jesus tells us about his relationship with God. He says, **"I and the Father are one."** God came to earth as a human being— as Jesus—to show us how much he loves us.

Let's thank God for coming to earth as Jesus and for preparing to show us how much God loves us. Dear God, thank you for coming to earth as a human being, as Jesus, to show us your love. In Jesus' name, amen.

# Satan Tempts Jesus

## Bible Story: Luke 4:1-13

Bible Verse: "Because he himself suffered when he was tempted, he is able to help those who are being tempted" (Hebrews 2:18).

**Simple Supplies:** *You'll need a Bible; tape; and, for each child, a craft stick, a red construction paper circle, and a green construction paper circle.*

Today we're going to learn about being tempted. Who can tell me what it means to be tempted? *Pause for children to respond.* When we're tempted, someone is trying to get us to do something that's wrong. Now we're going to play a game to help us learn more about temptations, and to play the game we each need to build a traffic light. *To each child, give a craft stick, a red circle, and a green circle. Show children how to tape a red circle to one end of the craft stick and a green circle to the other end. Pass around the tape, and help the children—especially the younger ones—tape together their traffic lights.*

*While the group is making the lights, continue with the message.* Did you know that even Jesus was tempted? Jesus was led into the desert to be tempted by the devil. Jesus was there a very long time without any food. What do you think that was like for Jesus? *Pause.* The devil tried to get Jesus to do three things. He tried to get Jesus to turn rocks into bread. He tried to get Jesus to worship him. He tried to get Jesus to prove he was the Son of God. Each time the devil tempted him to do these things, Jesus thought about what God's Word, the Bible, said to do. Each time, Jesus told the devil he wouldn't do what the devil asked. He told the devil "no." Why do you think God's Word helped Jesus when he was tempted? How can you remember God's Word when someone is asking you to do something wrong? *Pause for responses.* Why do you think Jesus was tempted? *Pause.* This is a hard question, so let's look to God's Word for the answer.

*Open your Bible to Hebrews 2:18, and show the page to the children.* Hebrews 2:18 says, **"Because he himself suffered when he was tempted, he is able to help those who are being tempted."** Jesus was tempted by the devil in the desert so that Jesus could help us do the right thing when we're tempted.

Let's play a game with the traffic lights we made. I'll make a suggestion to you; if it's OK to do what I'm suggesting, hold up your green lights. But if what I'm suggesting is a temptation that we should say "no" to, hold up your red lights. Ready?

*Mix tempting suggestions with suggestions that would be OK for kids to do— "It's OK if I don't tell my parents the truth," and "I really like to help my parents by making my bed", for example. Don't call attention to children who hold up the "incorrect" light, but do ask questions as you go along to help children understand what it means to be tempted.*

We face a lot of temptations! But because of his experience with the devil in the desert, Jesus knows exactly what being tempted feels like, and he can help us do the right thing. What do you think you should do when you're tempted to do wrong things? *Pause for responses.* When Jesus was tempted, he remembered what God's Word said. We can also pray and ask God for the wisdom and strength to do the right thing.

Let's thank God for helping us. Dear Jesus, we thank you for going through temptation yourself so that you can help us when we're tempted. Thank you for the Bible, which helps us know right from wrong. Please give us the wisdom and strength to do what is right. In your name, amen.

Take your lights home to remind you to ask God for help when you're tempted.

# Jesus Performs His First Miracle

## Bible Story: John 2:1-11

Bible Verse: "But these are written that you may believe that Jesus is the Christ, the Son of God, and that by believing you may have life in his name" (John 20:31).

**Simple Supplies:** *You'll need a Bible and a blanket big enough for four children to stand behind and not be seen.*

Sometimes it's hard to get to know people. At times we have to look closely for clues to help us know them better. What things do you do to get to know a person better? *Pause for responses.* Let's look for clues and see if you can guess who is who.

*Have the children form groups of three or four. Make sure that each group has an older child. Then choose one group to come forward. Tell the remaining groups to turn around so they can't see the chosen group.*

*Have the chosen group's members hold the blanket in front of them so that only their feet are visible below the blanket. Tell the other groups to turn back around.* Try to guess the identity of each child behind the blanket. *Switch groups, and repeat the activity. Try to give everyone a chance to stand behind the blanket. Afterward spread the blanket on the floor and have children sit around the edge.*

What clues helped you know who was behind the blanket? What was it like trying to guess who was who?

Jesus didn't look any different from other men, but Jesus did special things that no one else could do. These special things, called miracles, helped people know that Jesus was God's Son. His first miracle happened at a wedding party. Jesus, his mother, and his disciples were there having a great time. But then they noticed that there wasn't anything more to drink.

Jesus' mother told him about the problem. Jesus decided to help out. He told the servants to fill some large jars with water. The servants put the water into the jars, but the water came out as wine. Jesus performed the miracle of turning the water into wine. The Bible tells us in John 20:31: **"But these are written that you may believe that Jesus is the Christ, the Son of God, and that by believing you may have life in his name."**

Jesus did miracles to help us believe that he is truly God's Son, who we can live with forever in heaven. What other things has God done to help you believe in Jesus? *Pause for responses.* Let's pray now and thank him for helping us to know who he is. Dear God, thank you so much for the miracles Jesus did which tells us Jesus was God's Son. Thank you for helping us to believe in Jesus. In Jesus' name, amen.

# Jesus Teaches in a Synagogue

## Bible Story: Luke 4:14-21

> **Bible Verse:** "For the Son of Man came to seek and to save what was lost" (Luke 19:10).

**Simple Supplies:** *You'll need a Bible and, for each child, a treat such as an individually wrapped piece of candy. Avoid small, hard candies which may be choking hazards for younger children. Place the treats in easy-to-find "hiding places" where the children will be sitting.*

Let's begin today with a little scavenger hunt. I've hidden some special treats in our worship area. I'd like you to look around and see if you can find a treat. If you find one, stop looking, come back here, and sit quietly. Don't eat your treat yet. *Encourage kids to look throughout the worship area for the treats you've hidden. If no one finds a treat after a few moments, call out a hint such as "They're hidden on the floor." As children find treats, make sure they stop looking, return, and sit quietly without eating the treats. Be sure every child finds a treat. Then let children enjoy their treats as you continue.*

In the Bible, Jesus told people he was looking for something—just the way you were looking for treats today. He went into a synagogue, where the people went to worship God. The people had been waiting for God to send someone to show them the way to heaven. They didn't know that Jesus was the one God had sent.

Jesus knew the people were waiting for the special someone God sent. He read Scripture from the Bible that talked about the person they were waiting for. Then he told the people, "I'm the one the Scripture is talking about."

*Open your Bible to Luke 19:10, and show the page to the children.* In Luke 19:10, Jesus told people why God sent him: **"For the Son of Man came to seek and to save what was lost."** Jesus came to show the way to heaven for people who didn't know what that way was, just as you were looking for the treats in this room. Who can tell me the way to heaven? *Pause for children to respond.* The only way to get to heaven is to trust in Jesus. If we believe that Jesus died to pay for the wrong things we've done and trust him to take us to heaven, he will!

After you found your treats, you brought them back here. When Jesus finds people who are lost, he shows them the way to heaven. Someday he'll take his followers to heaven to be with him forever. Let's thank Jesus for showing us the way to heaven. Thank you, Jesus, for coming to earth, finding us when we were lost, and showing us the way to heaven. In your name, amen.

When do the kids get to eat their treats?

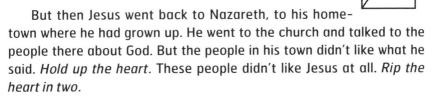

# Jesus Is Rejected in His Hometown

## Bible Story: Luke 4:22-30

> **Bible Verse:** "Love the Lord your God with all your heart and with all your soul and with all your strength" (Deuteronomy 6:5).

**Simple Supplies:** *You'll need a Bible, red construction paper, children's scissors, crayons, and colored markers. Before this sermon, fold sheets of red construction paper in half horizontally. You'll need one folded paper for every child, plus one for yourself. On each sheet of folded paper, draw half a heart shape so that when the sheet is opened, you'll have a whole heart.*

I'm glad you came today to learn about Jesus. In today's Bible story, Jesus had been preaching to the people throughout the land. He taught the people how much God loved them. *Hold up one folded sheet of paper.* All the people who heard Jesus liked him and said good things about him. *Cut on the line, then unfold the paper and show children the heart.*

But then Jesus went back to Nazareth, to his hometown where he had grown up. He went to the church and talked to the people there about God. But the people in his town didn't like what he said. *Hold up the heart.* These people didn't like Jesus at all. *Rip the heart in two.*

If Jesus came to our town today, how would you feel? What would you say to Jesus when you saw him? How would you treat Jesus if he walked into our church right now? *Pause for children to respond.*

45

*Open your Bible to Deuteronomy 6:5, and show the page to the children.* Deuteronomy 6:5 tells us how we should treat Jesus: **"Love the Lord your God with all your heart and with all your soul and with all your strength."** *Give each child one of the folded sheets of paper you prepared earlier. Set out children's scissors, crayons, and colored markers.* What does it mean to love Jesus with all your heart? *Pause to let children answer.* When you love someone with all your heart, you love them a whole bunch—more than anyone! Cut along the line on your paper to make a heart to show Jesus how much you love him. *Be prepared to help younger children cut their hearts.*

What do you think it means to love Jesus will all your soul? *Pause.* To love someone with all your soul means that all of you loves Jesus—you love him with your heart, and your brain, and all of your feelings. Write one word on your heart that shows how you feel about Jesus. *Pause as kids write. Be prepared to help younger children with spelling, and suggest words such as "love," "happy," or "thankful" if kids need help getting started.*

Our Bible verse says we should love Jesus with all our strength. What do you think that means? *Pause.* Loving Jesus with all our strength means that we should try really hard not to let anything get in the way of loving him. Let's close these paper hearts to show that we won't let anything come between us and Jesus. *After kids close their paper hearts, conclude in prayer.*

Before we go, let's pray: Dear God, thank you for loving us. And help us to love you with all our hearts, and all our souls, and all our strength. We love you. In Jesus' name, amen.

# fishermen Are Astonished by Miraculous catch

### Bible Story: Luke 5:1–11

> **Bible Verse: "If you love me, you will obey what I command"**
> **(John 14:15).**

**Simple Supplies:** *You'll need a Bible, several volunteers in the congregation, and plastic sandwich bags of small cookies. Before the* *message, give the bags of cookies to the volunteers. Explain how the message will proceed, and make sure the volunteers understand not to give children the cookies until the second time you send them into the worship area.*

Have you ever been fishing? What was it like? *Pause for children to respond.* Did you know that the Bible tells fishing stories? In Luke 5, the Bible tells about some fishermen who had been trying to catch fish. But the fish don't always do what we want them to, do they? Let's see what that was like for the fishermen in the Bible.

I'm going to send you into our congregation with a job to do: I want you to find a treat for the group to eat. *Ask several children to stand up and walk clockwise around the worship area. Ask other children to stand up and hop on their right feet to the middle of the worship area and back. Then ask a third group of kids to go into the congregation, shake hands with congregation members, and come back. The children should come back empty-handed.*

Did you find anything good out there? Well, that's OK. That really is similar to what happened to the fishermen. They had fished all night and hadn't caught a single fish—not one! They were probably tired and frustrated. Show me what your face looks like if you are tired and frustrated. *Have kids show their faces.*

When the fishermen were back on shore, getting ready to go home, Jesus came along. He wanted to sit in the boat and teach a crowd of people who were standing on the shore. When Jesus was finished teaching the people, he told Simon, a fisherman, to move the boat to deep water and drop the nets again. If you'd been fishing all night and hadn't caught anything, what would you think about this? *Pause.* Maybe Simon thought Jesus didn't know how to fish. Maybe Simon was unsure and a little annoyed. Show me what your face looks like if you are unsure and annoyed. *Have kids show their faces.*

To find out what happened to Simon, do again the jobs that I gave you at the beginning of the message. See if you can find a treat this time. *Ask several children to stand up and walk counterclockwise around the worship area. Ask other children to stand up and hop on their left feet to the middle of the worship area and back. Then ask a third group of kids to go into the congregation, shake hands with congregation members, and come back. This time, the volunteers should give some of the children the bags of cookies.*

Wow! You found some treats this time! Did you think you would? How did you feel about doing the jobs I gave you a second time? Why did you decide to obey and do what I asked you to do? *Pause for responses.*

You know, a very similar thing happened to Simon. He may not have understood why Jesus wanted the fishermen to go fishing again, but Simon decided to obey Jesus. They caught lots of fish—so many that their nets were about to break! They were amazed and very glad they had obeyed Jesus. Show me what your face looks like if you are amazed and glad. *Have kids show their faces.*

You obeyed my strange instructions, and now we all have a treat to eat. Simon obeyed Jesus' instructions and the fishermen caught lots and lots of fish. *Distribute the cookies to the children.* Isn't that a good feeling? What would have happened to our treat if you hadn't obeyed my instructions? *Pause.*

Let's see what Jesus says about why we should obey him. *Open your Bible to John 14:15, and show the page to the children.* In John 14:15, Jesus says, **"If you love me, you will obey what I command."** What do you think this verse means? *Pause.* If we love Jesus, we do as he says.

Let's pray together. God, sometimes we may not understand the things you ask us to do, or we may think those things are a little strange. But because we love you, we want to obey you. Please help us to always do as you say. In Jesus' name, amen.

# Jesus Teaches About Rewards

## Bible Story: Luke 6:17-26

> **Bible Verse: "Set your minds on things above, not on earthly things" (Colossians 3:2).**

**Simple Supplies:** *You'll need a Bible, a volunteer, a flashlight, and happy-face stickers.*

**W**elcome! To start today, I'd like you to find a partner to talk with. I'll let you know what to talk about. *Give kids a few moments to find a partner. You might want to help younger children with this* *task*. Great! Now I'd like you to tell your partner about one thing that makes you feel really good. *Give kids a few moments to talk.* Now I'd like you to tell your partner about one thing that makes you feel sad. *Give children a few moments to talk.*

Now that you've talked about your happy and sad times, I'd like you to choose one of those feelings to act out. And I want you to do the acting out without talking. *If children need help, suggest that they smile or frown or pretend to cry or laugh.*

Keep acting out your feelings. Next I'm going to come to each one of you and say, "Jesus loves you!" When I say that to you, I want you to stop acting out your feelings and walk around smiling at everyone. I'd like you to shake hands with three other people here. *Give each child a hug and say, "Jesus loves you." Have children walk around for a few moments, then call them back together.*

What happened when I told you that Jesus loves you? Which do you like better—acting unhappy or acting happy? Why? *Pause for responses.*

In the Bible, Jesus says he loves us all the time—when we're happy, and when we're sad. He also tells us that even if we're poor, hungry, sad, and lonely, we can be one hundred percent sure that Jesus loves us. When we feel bad, we can remember the good news that someday we'll get to be with Jesus in heaven.

*Open your Bible to Colossians 3:2, and show the page to the children.* Colossians 3:2 says, **"Set your minds on things above, not on earthly things."** If we give our attention to Jesus, we'll remember that Jesus loves us and that we can look forward to being with him in heaven. I'd like to show you how we can always remember Jesus' love, even when we're upset.

*Have children gather around you. Ask your volunteer to turn off the lights. Then turn on your flashlight.* How would you feel if you walked around in darkness all the time? *Pause for responses. Point the flashlight toward the ceiling.* Do you see the light? When the Bible tells us to set our minds on things above, it's telling us that no matter how unfriendly things around us seem to be, we should keep our eyes on Jesus—just as you're keeping your eyes on the light above us right now.

Let's pray and ask God to help us keep our eyes on him. Dear Lord, thank you for loving us and for giving us a chance to live with you in heaven. Your love makes us very happy. Help us keep our eyes on you so we'll remember your love all the time. In Jesus' name, amen.

I have some happy-face stickers to give you today. When you look at your stickers, remember to focus on the fact that Jesus loves you. *Give each child a sticker as they head back to their seats.*

# Jesus Teaches About Loving Enemies

## Bible Story: Luke 6:27-38

 Bible Verse: "Do to others as you would have them do to you" (Luke 6:31).

**Simple Supplies:** *You'll need a Bible; a paper bag; and three to five items children would like as presents—for example, a stuffed animal, a toy car or truck, a video game, and so on. Try to include an item older children would like as well as an item younger children would like. Place the items in the paper bag.*

Today I want to talk to you about love and the way we treat others. I have some items to show you, and I'd like you to silently think about which item you like best of all. In other words, which one of these items would you like to get as a present? *Pull the items out of the bag and place them in front of the group. Encourage kids to talk about the items.* Which of these do you like best? Which would you want to have? Why? *Pause for children to respond.*

OK, so now we know what we would choose for ourselves. But let's think about our good friends. How do you feel about your good friends? Tell us a little about your good friends. *Pause as children share.* Pretend that one of your good friends is having a birthday party and has invited you. Which one of these things would you want to give to your friend? Why? *Pause.*

Now let's go one step further. Think of someone who you don't get along with very well, but don't tell us who you're thinking about. Do you love this person you're thinking about? *Pause.* Pretend that this person has invited you to a birthday party. Which of these things would you want to give to that person?

I know exactly how you feel. Sometimes when people aren't nice to us, we don't want to be nice to them or give them the kinds of things we would like. But the Bible tells how we should treat all people—whether they're our good friends or people who don't treat us very nicely.

*Open your Bible to Luke 6:31, and show the page to the children.*  Listen to what Jesus said in Luke 6:31: **"Do to others as you would have them do to you."** What do you think this means? According to what the Bible says, if someone is being mean to you, how should you treat that person? *Pause.* We should always treat people the way we want to be treated. We like to be treated with kindness and love, so we should treat others with kindness and love.

Remember at the beginning of the message when we chose the gifts we liked best? If you were treating even your enemies as you like to be treated, what gift would you take to them? *Pause.* Even to someone who isn't very nice to us, we should give the kind of gift we'd like to have. That can be a hard thing to do, but we should do it anyway. Would  you all repeat this Bible verse with me please? **"Do to others as you would have them do to you."**

Let's close in prayer. I'll start the prayer, then I'll give you a few moments of quiet to think about the people you don't get along with very well. Ask God to help you be more kind and loving to those people, no  matter how hard it is for you. Dear God, thank you so much for teaching us about loving our enemies. Sometimes we have a very hard time loving our enemies, so please help each of us treat others as we want to be treated. *Pause for a few moments to let the children pray silently.* In Jesus' name, amen.

# Jesus Teaches About Good Fruit

## Bible Story: Luke 6:43-44

> **Bible Verse: "In the same way, let your light shine before men, that they may see your good deeds and praise your Father in heaven" (Matthew 5:16).**

**Simple Supplies:** *You'll need a Bible; a volunteer to turn off and on the* *lights; a flashlight; and a basket or platter of fruit such as apples, grapes, and bananas.*

Sit with children in a circle on the floor, and place the fruit in the center of the circle. How many of you like to eat fruit? *Pause for kids to respond.* Today our Bible story has to do with fruit. *Hold up an apple.* What kind of plant does this apple come from? this banana? these grapes? *Pause for kids to respond.*

Each kind of fruit comes from its own kind of plant. Jesus said that a good tree makes good fruit and a bad tree makes bad fruit. But Jesus wasn't really talking about fruit; he was talking about people! Jesus wants us to be good people and do good things in the very same way that good trees make good fruit.

Why do you think it's important for us to do good things? *Pause for children to respond.* There are lots of good reasons to do good things, and Matthew 5:16 tells us one good reason. *Open your Bible to Matthew 5:16, and show the page to the children.* This Scripture says, **"In the same way, let your light shine before men, that they may see your good deeds and praise your Father in heaven."** When we do good things, people learn about God's love. When we do good things, people thank and praise God.

*Hold up an apple again.* When people see a good apple, they know it came from a good apple tree. And when people see us do good things, they know we're sharing God's love. Jesus wants the good things we do to shine like lights so everyone can see them and praise God.

What good things can you do this week to show others that you love God? *Pause for children to respond.* We can pick up our rooms without being told, we can share with others—we can do all kinds of good things! Now I'll give you a moment to think about one good thing you will do during the coming week. *Pause.*

Jesus says we should let our good deeds shine like lights. *Turn on the flashlight.* I'm going to have my helper turn off the lights for a minute, and we'll pass the flashlight around the group. When the flashlight comes to you, say the good thing you'll do this week, then pass the flashlight to the next person. I'll start. *Have your helper turn off the lights. Then say a good deed that you will do in the coming week, and pass the flashlight to a child. Be sure each child who wants to share gets a chance to.*

Let's ask Jesus to help us shine like lights. Dear God, please help us shine like lights so others can see how much you love them through the good things we do. In Jesus' name, amen.

*Have the helper turn the lights back on, and close by having kids lead the congregation in singing "This Little Light of Mine."*

SECTION
# THREE

# SPRING
## QUARTER

# Jesus Teaches His Disciples to Pray

## Bible Story: Matthew 6:5-13

Bible Verse: "This, then, is how you should pray: 'Our Father in heaven, hallowed be your name, your kingdom come, your will be done on earth as it is in heaven. Give us today our daily bread. Forgive us our debts, as we also have forgiven our debtors. And lead us not into temptation, but deliver us from the evil one' " (Matthew 6:9-13).

**Simple Supplies:** *You'll need a Bible, a golf club, and a plastic golf ball.*

How many of you have ever played golf? Did you like it? *Ask several children to share their stories of golfing.* I'm not a very good golfer, but don't tell anyone I admitted that. Still, I think I'm good enough to teach most of you a few things. So this morning I'm going to give you a quick golf lesson—and you don't even have to pay me for it.

*Hold up the golf ball.* The first thing you need to know is that this is a golf ball. *Hold up the golf club.* And this is a golf club. The idea is to put the ball on the ground and then use the club to hit the ball a long way away into a little tiny hole in the ground. Let's pretend the hole is back there behind the back row. OK. Here's what you do. You get in position to hit the ball...*tee up, facing the audience*...you wiggle a little bit to loosen up...*do so*...then you take a big swing and hit the ball...*swing and miss*. Where did it go? Did it go into the cup?

*When children point out that the ball hasn't moved, go through the process again. Then with a shrug, put down the club and pick up your Bible.*

Nobody would want to take golf lessons from me, would they? Why? Right—because I can't even hit the ball! It's hard to teach someone how to golf when you don't do it very well yourself. When it comes to teaching, we all want teachers who know what they're doing!

That's why when we want to learn how to pray, we want a teacher like Jesus. Jesus gave us a lesson about how to pray in Matthew 6. *Open your Bible to Matthew 6:9-13 and show the page to the children.* Jesus said praying was important. God wants us to pray and tell him what's going on every day. And he wants to help us learn things about him and how to live, too.

But sometimes people don't do that. Sometimes they forget to respect God when they pray. Or they ask for things God doesn't want them to have. Or they ask for forgiveness, but they don't forgive others. So Jesus taught about prayer.

Sometimes this prayer is called the Lord's Prayer, but it's really a lesson about how to pray. Maybe you know it. *Speak to the audience.* Maybe you know it, too. Let's all repeat it as I say it. " **'Our Father in heaven,**  **hallowed be your name, your kingdom come, your will be done on earth as it is in heaven. Give us today our daily bread. Forgive us our debts, as we also have forgiven our debtors. And lead us not into temptation, but deliver us from the evil one.' "** *Many members of your congregation may have learned the King James Version of this passage. If so, repeat it with them, and then read it again in the child-friendlier New International Version above.* The prayer Jesus taught worships God; tells God that we understand he's in charge; and asks God to provide for us, to forgive us as we forgive others, and to protect us.

Please close your eyes and bow your heads, and let's pray. As we pray I'll help us understand what the words we are praying mean.

Our Father...
*God, you are our Father. You love us and want us to be your children.*
Our Father in heaven, hallowed be your name...
*You are holy, God. You alone are perfect and without sin.*
Your kingdom come, your will be done on earth as it is in heaven.
*We want to do what you want us to do. Please help us know what you want.*
Give us today our daily bread.
*Thank you for taking good care of us today, God.*
Forgive us our debts as we have forgiven our debtors.
*Thank you for forgiving us for the wrong things we do, God. Please help us to forgive others the way you forgive us.*
And lead us not into temptation, but deliver us from the evil one.
*We want to do what's right, God. Please help us.*
In Jesus' name, amen.

Jesus is the greatest teacher ever, and he knows about talking with God, his Father. Let's remember what Jesus taught us.

And do you mind if I try this once more? *Tee up again and gently waft the plastic ball toward the back of the room. Then dismiss the children.*

# Moses and Elijah Appear With Jesus

### Bible Story: Luke 9:28-36

> **Bible Verse:** "The Word became flesh and made his dwelling among us. We have seen his glory, the glory of the One and Only, who came from the Father, full of grace and truth" (John 1:14).

**Simple Supplies:** *You'll need a Bible.*

Please find a partner. *Help kids form pairs. You may want to encourage younger children to pair up with older children. If some children are hesitant to form pairs, allow those children to be your partners.* Now spend a few moments talking with your partner. A little later, I'm going to ask you to tell the rest of the group about your partner. So you want to find out your partner's name and one thing he or she likes to do. *Allow children to talk for thirty to sixty seconds.*

This reminds me of something that happened to Jesus' disciples. God wanted to tell the disciples who Jesus was. So once when Jesus and three of his disciples were praying on a mountain, Jesus suddenly looked like he was shining. Then two other men appeared, and they talked with Jesus.

Now the interesting thing about the two men who appeared is that they had lived a long, long time before Jesus was on earth. Perhaps you'll recognize their names: one man was Moses, who led the Israelites out of Egypt, and the other man was Elijah, one of God's great prophets. Moses and Elijah were heroes to the disciples. And even though Moses and Elijah had died long ago, they were standing right in front of the disciples and they were talking to Jesus! How do you think the disciples felt about that? *Pause.*

As Jesus was talking to Moses and Elijah, a cloud surrounded Jesus and the disciples. Then they heard God speaking in a voice that came from the cloud. God said, "This is my Son, whom I have chosen; listen to him."

So you see, God told the disciples who Jesus was. First he showed the disciples that Jesus was special by making him shine. Then he showed Jesus talking with two of the greatest men the disciples had ever heard of. By doing this God wanted the disciples to know that Jesus was God's

Son and that they should listen to what Jesus said. God told the disciples who Jesus was, and you can tell others who Jesus is, too. But first let's tell each other about the friends we talked to at the beginning of the message. *Have children each take a turn telling their partner's name and one thing their partner likes to do. Help younger children tell about their partners. If you have more than twelve children, have pairs from groups of four and tell about each other in the small groups.*

Just as you told the group about each other, you can tell others who Jesus is. How can you tell others who Jesus is? *Pause.* Find your partner again, and practice telling each other one thing you know about Jesus. For example, you might say, "I know Jesus loves us" or "I know Jesus is God's Son." *Pause.*

*Open your Bible to John 1:14, and show the page to the children.* John 1:14 tells us about Jesus: **"The Word became flesh and made his dwelling among us. We have seen his glory, the glory of the One and Only, who came from the Father, full of grace and truth."** God told us that Jesus is his Son, and Jesus came to earth—became flesh— to tell us about God.

Let's pray. Dear God, thank you for sending your Son, Jesus, to earth to show us what you're like. Thank you for telling us who he is so that we know we should listen to him. In Jesus' name, amen.

*Encourage children each to tell at least one person about Jesus during the week, then have them return to their seats.*

---

# Zacchaeus Climbs a Tree to See Jesus

## Bible Story: Luke 19:1–10

> Bible Verse: "Here I am! I stand at the door and knock. If anyone hears my voice and opens the door, I will come in and eat with him, and he with me" (Revelation 3:20).

**Simple Supplies:** *You'll need a Bible and several adult volunteers from the congregation. Before the message, talk to your volunteers about*

*what will happen during the message. Ask them if you can borrow some-thing from them—a watch, a purse, or a hat, for example. Assure them that you'll return the items, unharmed, during the message. Also encour-age them to complain or protest while they're giving the items to you.*

Have the children meet you at the back of the room. Hello, everyone! I thought we'd begin by going on a little walk. We're going to talk about a man named Zacchaeus and his experience with Jesus. Let's pretend that I'm Zacchaeus. *Bend down or "walk" on your knees so you're short like Zacchaeus.* I'm a short man. I'm a tax collector. I take money from people to give to the government. *Begin walking toward the front of the room. As you walk past your volunteers, say things like,* "Well, [name of person], I think you owe the government. Give me something valuable for the government. And throw in some extra for me. You know, for the effort."

*Lead the children to the worship area, then lay the items you col-lected on the floor.* Boy, we've sure got a lot of stuff here! But I don't think those people were very happy with me, do you? It seemed to me like they were a little mad. Why do you suppose that is? *Pause for re-sponses.* Yeah, I guess I do take more than I'm supposed to. To most people, I guess I'm not a very nice person.

But I have problems, too! I mean, look at how short I am! Jesus is coming to our town, and I'm so short that I won't even be able to see him!

OK. Let's pretend that you all are the townspeople and that Jesus is coming to our town today. *Have the children stand and crowd around you so you're hidden from the congregation.* I've heard a lot about Jesus and would really like to see him, but I can't see a thing! What should I do? *Pause for responses.* Ah, I should climb a tree! *Stand up tall, and have the children sit down.* That's good! Now I can see!

Do you know what happened next to Zacchaeus? *Pause.* Jesus saw Zacchaeus in the tree and told him, "Come down right away. I must stay at your house today." When Jesus reached out to Zacchaeus, he felt loved for the first time in a long time. Jesus' love changed Zacchaeus. Zacchaeus changed so much that he gave the people their things back. Plus more! *Hand back the items you borrowed from your volunteers. As you do so, say things like, "I've learned my lesson. I won't cheat anyone again. I'll pay you back four times what I've taken from you!" When you've handed back all the items, join the children again.*

Why do you think Zacchaeus changed? How do you feel when someone shows love to you? *Pause for children to respond. Then open* your Bible to Revelation 3:20, and show the page to the children. Now listen to what Revelation 3:20 says: **"Here I am! I stand at the door and knock. If anyone hears my voice and opens the door, I will come in and eat with him, and he with me."** How did Jesus knock at Zacchaeus' door? How did Zacchaeus open the door? What happened to Zacchaeus when he welcomed Jesus into his heart? *Pause for responses.* Just as Jesus called out to Zacchaeus, he calls out to us. He loves us and wants us to let him into our hearts. When we decide to love Jesus, he lives in our hearts. And we can live with him forever in heaven.

Let's pray. Dear Jesus, thank you for loving each of us so much that you call to us and knock at the doors to our hearts. Thank you for giving each of us the chance to love you, too. In Jesus' name, amen.

# Jesus Tells the Parable of the Lost Son

## Bible Story: Luke 15:11-32

> **Bible Verse: "But you are a forgiving God, gracious and compassionate, slow to anger and abounding in love" (Nehemiah 9:17b).**

**Simple Supplies:** *You'll need a Bible and streamers.*

Help children get into three different groups. *It's OK to have one or two children in each group.* Have any of you ever been lost? What was it like? *Pause for children to respond.* Jesus told a story about a young man who was lost. I'd like to tell you that story, but I'll need your help. *Point to one group of children.* Whenever I say the word "money," I'd like you to yell "cha-ching!" *Have the group practice, then point to a second group of children.* When I say the word "party," I'd like you to yell "whoo-hoo!" *Have the group practice, then point to a third group of children.* When I say the word "father," I'd like you to say, "I love you!" *Have the group practice.* Everyone ready?

*As you read the following synopsis, help groups remember their lines.* Jesus told a story about a **father** who had two sons. One day, the younger son said to his **father**, "Give me my share of your **money**."

Now, that was not a nice thing to do. *Throw streamers on the group.* The **father** gave the son the **money**, and then the son left his **father's** house. *Throw more streamers on the kids.* The son spent lots and lots of **money** on bad things that his **father** didn't approve of. *Throw more streamers.* The son went to **parties** every day. He kept spending his **money**. *Throw the last of the streamers on the kids. They should be fairly covered in streamers.* Soon, the son didn't have any **money** left— not even a penny. To make enough **money** to eat, the son got a job feeding pigs. That was no **party**! The son was so hungry that he thought about eating the pigs' food! What do you think the son should do? Why? *Pause for responses.* What would you do if you were the son and you were starving? *Allow children to respond.* Well, the son decided that he should return to his **father** even though he had spent all the **money**. As he walked home, he thought a lot about what to say to his **father**. What do you think he should say? *Pause.* The son decided he had behaved very badly and needed to ask his **father** to forgive him.

Now before we hear the end of Jesus' story, I'd like you to look around. What's it like to be covered with streamers? *Pause.* It's kind of like being covered with sin, isn't it? When we do wrong things, they fill up our lives and make us messy and build a wall between us and our heavenly Father. To remove the messy covering of sin, we need our heavenly Father's forgiveness.

Now let's go back to the story. The son had decided to ask his **father** for forgiveness. As the son was walking home, his **father** saw him. What do you think the **father** thought about his son at that point? *Pause.* The **father** ran to his son, hugged him, and kissed him. Then the son said, "**Father** I have done so many wrong things. I'm sorry." And do you know what? The **father**, who had never stopped loving his son, forgave him and threw a **party** to welcome him home.

Jesus told this story to teach us about God's forgiveness. *Open your Bible to Nehemiah 9:17b, and show the page to the children.* Listen to what the Bible says in Nehemiah 9:17b: "**But you are a forgiving God, gracious and compassionate, slow to anger and abounding in love.**" Even when we do wrong things, God loves us. When we're covered in sin, God wants us to ask him to remove that sin so we can have a good relationship with him. When we remove our sin, God is just as happy as the father in Jesus' story. Let's celebrate God's forgiveness by standing up, removing the streamers, and throwing them around like we're having a party. *Give children time to celebrate, and help them toss the streamers around. After a few moments, ask the children to sit down again.*

Let's thank God for his love and forgiveness. First think of some-thing you've done that you shouldn't have done. During our prayer, I'll pause so you can silently ask God to forgive you for that sin. Dear God, we are so happy and thankful that you love us so very much. We love you, too, and we want to ask for your forgiveness now. *Pause for a minute so children can pray silently.* God, thank you for cleaning away our messy sins. In Jesus' name, amen.

# Jesus Washes the Disciples' Feet

## Bible Story: John 13:1-17

Bible Verse: "If anyone wants to be first, he must be the very last, and the servant of all" (Mark 9:35b).

**Simple Supplies:** *You'll need a Bible, napkins, a plate, cookies, and plastic sandwich bags. You'll need two cookies for each child. Put each cookie in a plastic bag, and place all the cookies on the plate.*

It's great to see you all today. I've brought a special treat with me. *Show children the plate of cookies.* Who would like one of these yummy cookies? *Pause for children to respond.* They sure look good, don't they? Before we enjoy these treats, I'd like to tell you about something Jesus said to his disciples.

Right before Jesus was arrested and crucified, he and his disciples were eating a special meal. Jesus did something very surprising: He washed all of the disciples' feet! In Bible times, people wore sandals and walked everywhere, so their feet got dusty and dirty. Usually a servant washed the feet of dinner guests, but Jesus wanted to serve others himself. He told his disciples that they should follow his example and be willing to serve others.

A verse in the Bible sums up what Jesus was trying to teach his dis-ciples that night. *Open your Bible to Mark 9:35, and show the page to the children.* Listen while I read what Jesus said in Mark 9:35: **"If anyone wants to be first, he must be the very last, and the servant of all."** What do you think that verse means? *Pause to let children answer.*

Jesus says we should serve others instead of trying to be first. Let's do something that I think will help you understand. *Hold up the plate of*

*cookies.* Let's serve others some cookies. *Have each child give a cookie and a napkin to someone in the congregation. Then have children gather back together.*

Thanks for serving those cookies. The way you served those cookies before eating them yourselves shows that you were willing to serve others. What other ways can you serve others? When can you serve others? *Pause for responses.* You know, that's just what Jesus tells us to do. Even though you really may have wanted to eat the cookies yourselves, you served others first. In a moment, I'll give each of you your own cookie. But first, let's pray.

Dear Jesus, thank you for teaching us how to serve others. Help us to always remember your example. In Jesus' name, amen.

*Give each child a cookie to take back to their seats.*

# Jesus Is Tried and Crucified

## Bible Story: Luke 19:28-40; 23:1-49

Bible Verse: "But God demonstrates his own love for us in this: While we were still sinners, Christ died for us" (Romans 5:8).

**Simple Supplies:** *You'll need a Bible and a cross. If your worship area contains a cross, just have the children initially meet you in front of the cross.*

Let's talk about love for a moment. How do we show people we love them? *Pause for children to respond. Encourage kids to brainstorm for several ideas.* Those are all great ways to show people we love them. Today I'm going to tell you a story from the Bible about how Jesus shows us he loves us.

The Bible tells us that God is perfect but that we aren't perfect. Sometimes we hurt people, tell lies, or take things that don't belong to us. Doing things like that harms our relationship with God.

We often use a cross shape to help us think of God. To see what happens with our relationship with God when we do bad things, let's use this cross to represent God. Let's all stand up. *Lead kids in standing and facing the cross.* I'll name some wrong things people do. Each time I name one of these sins, you should take a step away from the cross. *Name several sins such as lying, being unkind, cheating, disobeying, and so on. Each time you name a sin, lead the group in taking a large step away from the cross.*

Look at the cross way over there. How have our sins changed how close we are to God? *Pause.* When we sin, we become separated from God. We don't want to be separated from God, and God doesn't want us to be apart from him, either. So God sent his Son, Jesus, to help us be close to God again.

This is how it happened. When Jesus came to earth, many people thought he would be a powerful king with lots of money, a big army, and maybe even a crown and a throne. So one day when Jesus rode a donkey into the city of Jerusalem, the people thought he was coming to take his place as the king. They celebrated and shouted praises and waved palm leaves. Jesus knew the people didn't understand why he had come down to earth from heaven, and he also knew what would happen to him next. He knew that very soon, those same people would be angry with him. *Lead children in taking another step away from the cross.*

Of course, Jesus was right. Just a little while later, the people were angry with Jesus for saying he was God's Son, and for not wanting to be a powerful earthly king. *Lead children in taking another step away from the cross.* But Jesus didn't run away and hide. He showed his love for us by letting the people treat him so horribly. *Lead children in taking another step away from the cross.* The people did very mean things to Jesus and finally they let him be killed. *For each offense, lead children in taking another step away from the cross.* Jesus was being punished for every single sin every single person in the world had ever committed and would ever commit. Jesus died for all sins. *Lead children in taking another step away from the cross.*

Do you know why Jesus took all of that punishment even though he had never done anything wrong? *Pause.* Jesus did these things to show us how much God loves us. We don't get the punishment we deserve when we sin because Jesus, who never sinned, was punished for us.

*Open your Bible to Romans 5:8, and show the page to the children.* Romans 5:8 tells us how Jesus shows us he loves us: "**But God demonstrates his own love for us in this: While we were still sinners, Christ died for us.**" God sent Jesus to take the punishment we deserve even though everyone sins and even though God knew people would still sin. This is how Jesus showed his love for us.

65

Now let's see what happened to our relationship with God because Jesus died for our sins. *Lead the kids in moving back to the cross, gathering around the cross as closely as possible.* See how close we are to the cross now? Well, because Jesus died for us, we can be even closer than this to God. We're not separated from God anymore. Isn't that great news? Wow! God must really love us! How can we thank God for loving us? How can we thank Jesus for dying on the cross for us? *Pause for children to respond.*

Let's thank Jesus right now in a prayer. Thank you, God, for loving us so much that you sent your Son, Jesus, to die for our sins. Thank you, Jesus, for dying so we can be close to God. In Jesus' name, amen.

We can also thank Jesus by loving other people. When you see people you love, be sure to show your love to them. Then tell them about Jesus' love.

# Jesus Appears to Mary

### Bible Story: John 20:1-18

> **Bible Verse:** "That if you confess with your mouth, 'Jesus is Lord,' and believe in your heart that God raised him from the dead, you will be saved" (Romans 10:9).

**Simple Supplies:** *You'll need a Bible, paper lunch sacks, and colored markers.*

L et's begin by telling everyone some good news. On the count of three, let's call out, "Jesus is alive!" Ready? One, two, three—Jesus is alive!

That is an important message. In fact, it's the most important message ever told! The Bible tells us that after Jesus died on the cross, a woman named Mary went to the tomb where they had put Jesus' body. This Mary wasn't Jesus' mother; this woman was another Mary. Jesus was a good friend of Mary's, so she was very sad he was dead. Show me your best sad face. *Pause as kids respond.* But while Mary was at Jesus' tomb, something amazing happened. She met Jesus himself! He had risen from the dead! He was alive! How do you think Mary felt? Show me with your faces how you think Mary felt. *Pause.* Mary was so surprised and so, so happy. She wanted to tell everyone the message that Jesus was alive. She ran to tell the disciples the important news. Let's make something to help us tell this important message to others.

*Give each child a paper lunch bag, still folded, and show kids how to draw a simple face on the bottom of the bag. Show kids how to draw the puppet's mouth along the area where the bottom edge of the bag is folded to meet the side of the bag. Then show kids how to place one hand inside the bag and work the puppet's "mouth."*

What might have happened if Mary had never told anyone else the good news about Jesus? How would you feel if no one had ever told you about Jesus? *Pause for children to respond.* Because we know and love Jesus, we can live with him forever in heaven. That's why telling others that Jesus is alive, just as Mary did, is so important. Listen to what the Bible says in Romans 10:9: **"If you confess with your mouth, 'Jesus is Lord,' and believe in your heart that God raised him from the dead, you will be saved."** Jesus lives in our hearts if we believe he's alive and say with our mouths that Jesus is Lord.

In just a moment, we're going to use our puppets to tell others that important message. But first let's thank God for raising Jesus from the dead so we can be saved. Dear God, thank you for raising Jesus from the dead. Please help us to tell others that Jesus is alive. In Jesus' name, amen.

Now let's stand and use our puppets to tell the congregation, "Jesus is alive!" *Have kids stand, wear their puppets, and shout out, "Jesus is alive!" Then, before sending kids back to their seats, encourage them to use their puppets to tell at least one person the important message that Jesus is alive.*

# The Apostles Defend Their Faith

## Bible Story: Acts 5:12-42

Bible Verse: "Consider it pure joy, my brothers, whenever you face trials of many kinds, because you know that the testing of your faith develops perseverance" (James 1:2-3).

**Simple Supplies:** *You'll need a Bible.*

67

Have you ever been put down or made fun of because you believe in Jesus? How did that feel? What did you do? *Pause for children to respond.*

The Bible says that some of the apostles, who were Jesus' followers, were teaching people about him. Some people called the Sadducees didn't like what the disciples were saying. These Sadducees didn't believe in Jesus, so they put the apostles into jail. If you knew that someone would make fun of you or get angry with you for talking about Jesus, would you do it anyway? Why or why not? *Pause.* Think about one important thing you would like to tell someone about Jesus. *Give kids a few moments to think.*

Now we're going to pretend that we're the apostles and the congregation is the Sadducees. We're going to tell the Sadducees what we believe about Jesus. I'll go first. *Stand and face the congregation.* I believe that Jesus is the Son of God. Who else wants to volunteer to tell the Sadducees what you believe? *Have volunteers stand and face the congregation, one at a time, and tell what they believe about Jesus. Don't force children to volunteer. To encourage children to volunteer, have groups of kids stand up and together tell the congregation, "I believe that Jesus is the Son of God" or "I believe that Jesus is alive."*

What was it like to tell what you believe about Jesus? *Pause for responses.* Even though we knew the congregation wouldn't throw us into jail or do anything mean to us, it can still be kind of scary to talk about Jesus in front of people. What happens to our faith when we tell others about Jesus? What happens to our faith when we do what Jesus wants us to do—even when it's scary? *Pause for responses.* It's good to remember what we believe about Jesus so we can tell others about him when the time is right.

How do you think the apostles felt about being thrown into jail? *Pause.* Let me read to you a verse that tells more about it, and we'll see if you can guess how the apostles felt. *Open your Bible to James 1:2-3, and show the page to the children.* James 1:2-3 says, **"Consider it pure joy, my brothers, whenever you face trials of many kinds, because you know that the testing of your faith develops perseverance."** We should be happy when we're treated badly for believing in Jesus. That's exactly how the apostles felt: happy! Why do you think they felt this way? Why do you think you should be happy when you're made fun of or put down because you believe in Jesus? *Pause.*

When we face bad times because of our faith, our faith actually grows stronger. That's why the apostles were happy; their faith grew

68

stronger. In the same way, your faith grew stronger when you faced the "Sadducees" in the congregation and told what you believe about Jesus.

Let's pray together. Dear God, thank you so much for helping our faith to grow stronger when we face difficult times. And please help us remember to be happy because our faith is growing. In Jesus' name, amen.

---

# Saul Meets Jesus Near Damascus

## Bible Story: Acts 9:1-20

> **Bible Verse:** "Therefore, if anyone is in Christ, he is a new creation; the old has gone, the new has come!" (2 Corinthians 5:17).

**Simple Supplies:** *You'll need a Bible and blankets or towels.*

How many of you have seen a caterpillar? What does it look like? *Pause for children to respond.* Show me how a caterpillar moves. *Allow children to show you.* There's something very special about caterpillars. Can you tell me what it is? *Pause for children to respond.* Caterpillars turn into butterflies!

Let's pretend that we're caterpillars turning into butterflies. *Give each child a blanket or towel.* Let's spin a cocoon around us. *Have children wrap the cloth around them.* Caterpillars stay in their cocoons for a long time; when they come out, they're no longer caterpillars but beautiful butterflies! *Have children unwrap themselves.* Show me how a beautiful butterfly moves. *Allow children to show you.*

You know, a man in the Bible named Saul was kind of like a caterpillar. The Bible says that Saul was mean to people who said they loved Jesus. In fact, he wanted to put into jail everyone who loved Jesus.

One day Saul was on his way to arrest some people who loved Jesus. A bright light flashed, and he fell down. He heard a voice say, "Saul, why are you being mean to me?" Saul asked, "Who are you?" The voice said, "I'm Jesus, who you're hurting! Now get up and go to the city. Then you'll be told what to do." When Saul got up, he couldn't see! He was kind of like the caterpillar wrapped up in the cocoon.

For three days, Saul couldn't see. He also didn't eat or drink anything. Then God sent a man named Ananias to see Saul. Ananias placed his hands on Saul; then scales fell from Saul's eyes, and he could see again! This was kind of like a butterfly coming out of its cocoon.

Saul had completely changed from hating Jesus and wanting to hurt people who followed him to loving Jesus and wanting to tell others about him.

The Bible says that each of us is like a caterpillar. *Open your Bible to 2 Corinthians 5:17, and show the page to the children.* Second Corinthians 5:17 says, **"Therefore, if anyone is in Christ, he is a new creation; the old has gone the new has come."** If you love Jesus, you don't act the way you used to, just as the butterfly no longer acts like a caterpillar.

Let's close our eyes and ask God to help us act like new creations. Thank you, God, for changing us and letting us become like beautiful butterflies! Help us to do what you want us to do. In Jesus' name, amen.

*Dismiss kids by letting them fly away like butterflies.*

# Peter Raises Tabitha from the Dead

## Bible Story: Acts 9:36-43

> **Bible Verse: "The prayer of a righteous man is powerful and effective" (James 5:16b).**

**Simple Supplies:** *You'll need a Bible, a piece of paper, tape, string, scissors, and a pen. Before the sermon, tear the piece of paper into two pieces, cut the string in half, and take apart the pen.*

Ask children to form three groups. *Give one group the torn piece of paper and some tape. Give the second group the two pieces of string. Give the third group the pen pieces.* I've given each group something that's broken and needs to be fixed. Please work in your group to fix it. *Pause to allow children to fix their items. If children need help, show them how to tape the paper, tie together the string, and put together the pen.* Great job, everyone! How did you fix your item? How difficult was it to fix? *Allow children to respond, then set aside the supplies.*

Today we're going to talk about a time that Peter, one of Jesus' disciples, was asked to fix something—something that was very, very difficult to fix. We'll see what Peter did.

One day some people came to ask Peter to travel with them to their town. A friend of theirs named Tabitha had been sick and had just died. Everyone loved Tabitha because she was always helping people. Why do you think the people loved Tabitha? How would you have felt if you'd been Tabitha's friend and you found out that she had died? *Pause.*

Peter went with the people, and they took him to where Tabitha's body was lying on a bed. Some of the people Tabitha had helped were there. They were crying and showing Peter the clothing Tabitha had made for them. How would you have felt if you were Peter? What would you have done? *Pause.*

At the beginning of our message, you easily fixed some things for me. But Peter had something much more difficult to fix! Do you know what Peter did? He sent everyone out of the room, then he got down on his knees to pray. Let's get on our knees now the way Peter did. What is prayer? Why do people pray? Why do you think Peter decided to pray right then? *Pause for children to respond.*

Peter trusted God to hear and answer his prayer. He knew what God's Word says about prayer. *Open your Bible to James 5:16b, and show the page to the children.* James 5:16b says, **"The prayer of a righteous man**  **is powerful and effective."** Peter knew that prayer was powerful, so he prayed to God about Tabitha. Then he turned to Tabitha and said, "Tabitha, get up." Suddenly, Tabitha opened her eyes! She looked at Peter and sat up. Peter took her hand and helped her get out of bed. Stand up now just as Tabitha did when Peter told her to.

How did Peter solve his problem? What does this story from the Bible tell you about prayer? about God? *Pause.* When has God answered a prayer for you? *Allow plenty of time for children to share their answered prayers. If necessary, help them remember by suggesting specific ideas, such as God healing a relative, providing something they needed, or taking care of them when they were afraid. Also remind children that God sometimes answers our prayers by telling us "no" or "not right now."*

*Have children form a circle.* Now we're going to spend some time praying just as Peter did. We'll take turns praying aloud about lots of things: things we need to ask God for, things we'd like to thank God for, or just things we want to talk to God about. Whoever wants to can pray. As we pray, remember: **"The prayer of a righteous man is powerful**

**and effective."** I'll start. Dear God, thank you for listening to our prayers. Here are some things we want to talk to you about today. *Present a specific prayer of your own. Then allow children to share prayers of their own.* Now we'll spend a few moments in silent prayer, talking to God about things that are just between him and us. *Allow several moments for silent prayer.* Thank you, God, for listening to and answering our prayers. In Jesus' name, amen.

Remember, just as God listened to and answered Peter's powerful prayer, God listens to and answers our prayers.

# An Angel frees Peter from Jail

### Bible Story: Acts 12:1-18

> **Bible Verse:** "For he will command his angels concerning you to guard you in all your ways" (Psalm 91:11).

**Simple Supplies:** *You'll need a Bible, three chairs, a leader of the church, and two other adult volunteers. Before the message, place two chairs in front of the other to represent a prison cell. Ask an adult in the church that the children recognize as an authority figure to play the part of Peter and two more adults to bring "Peter" to the prison and stand guard at the beginning of the message. Explain the volunteers' roles, and especially make sure Peter understands his line. If costumes are available, use them to add to the realism of the message.*

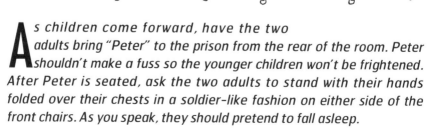

**A**s children come forward, have the two adults bring "Peter" to the prison from the rear of the room. Peter shouldn't make a fuss so the younger children won't be frightened. After Peter is seated, ask the two adults to stand with their hands folded over their chests in a soldier-like fashion on either side of the front chairs. As you speak, they should pretend to fall asleep.

Hi, children. Sorry about all of the commotion. What do you think is happening? *Pause for the children to respond.* They put this man in jail, didn't they? I wonder what this man did. Let's ask him.

*If you have a child who's willing to ask Peter what he did, have the child do so. Otherwise, ask Peter yourself.* Excuse me, sir. We're very curious to know why you're in prison. Would you mind telling us what happened?

*Have Peter respond that his name is Peter and that he was telling everyone about Jesus but that the king didn't like it and put him in prison.*

Wow, you made the king angry. I'd be scared if I were you. *Address the children again, and have Peter get down on his knees and pray.* So Peter was put into jail because he was telling people about Jesus. Do you know that even today people in some places can get into trouble for telling others about Jesus? The Bible says Peter's friends prayed for him when he was in jail, and we can pray for people today who are in trouble for loving Jesus, too. Let's say a prayer right now for those people. Dear God, we know that people all over the world are in trouble because they love Jesus and want to tell others about him. Please help those people to be brave, and please send help to them. In Jesus' name, amen.

In the Bible, God promises to help us when we're in the kind of trouble Peter's in. *Open your Bible to Psalm 91:11, and show the page to the children.* In Psalm 91:11 the Bible says, **"For he will command his angels concerning you to guard you in all your ways."** God's angels will guard us! What do you think about God's promise? *Pause for responses.* Isn't it nice to know that God's angels are watching over us?

I have a great idea! Let's pretend that we are God's angels, and we've been sent to free Peter from jail. We'll have to be quiet so the guards don't know we're here. *Have children huddle together.* Let's quietly surround Peter, take his hands, and then take him out of jail. *Lead kids in helping Peter out of jail. Once Peter is free, have him thank the "angels" and then hurry off to tell his friends what happened.*

All right! You did it! You guys did a great job! You know, the Bible tells us that angels really did help Peter get out of jail, just as God promised. I want you to remember that God is always watching over you. Just as the Bible said, God has commanded his angels to protect you. Let's thank God. Dear God, thank you so much for your protection. Thank you for sending your angels to help us. We know that we can feel brave and tell others about you because you're always with us. In Jesus' name, amen.

# Lydia's Conversion

### Bible Story: Acts 16:9-15

Bible Verse: "Preach the Word; be prepared in season and out of season" (2 Timothy 4:2a).

**Simple Supplies:** *You'll need Bibles, mittens, umbrellas, and sunglasses.*

*ave the children form a circle, and place all the supplies in the middle of the circle.* I brought some things today that help us to be prepared for different weather. What does it mean to be prepared? *Pause for responses.* When we're prepared, we're ready. Show me what you need to be prepared for cold, snowy weather. *Choose several children to stand and hold up the mittens. Then have the children sit down.* Now show me what you need to be prepared for rainy weather. *Choose different children to stand and hold up the umbrellas. Then have children sit back down.* And what do we need to be prepared for sunny weather? *Choose children to stand and hold up the sunglasses. Then have children sit back down.* Now finally, what do we need in order to be prepared to tell people about Jesus? *Choose children to stand up and hold up the Bibles. Take one of the Bibles, then have the children sit back down.*

Thanks for your help, everyone! Let's read what the Bible says about being prepared to tell people about Jesus. *Open the Bible to 2 Timothy 4:2a, and show the page to the children.* Second Timothy 4:2a says: **"Preach the Word; be prepared in season and out of season."** No matter what season it is—winter *(hold up a mitten)*, spring *(hold up an umbrella)*, summer *(hold up a pair of sunglasses)*, or fall *(hold up an umbrella again)*—we need to be prepared to tell people about Jesus *(hold up the Bible)*. Why should we tell others about Jesus? How can we tell others about Jesus? *Pause.*

The Bible tells us how the Apostle Paul told people about Jesus. Paul had a dream in which a man from a country called Macedonia asked for his help. Paul was prepared. He went to Macedonia right away and told the people about Jesus. If you met people who had never heard of Jesus, what would you tell them about him? Find a partner, and pretend that you're Paul telling about Jesus. For example, you can tell your partner that Jesus loves us or that Jesus shows us how to live. *Help children find partners and tell their partners about Jesus.*

A woman named Lydia lived in Macedonia, and she listened to what Paul said about Jesus. She believed it was true, so she and everyone in her household were baptized. That's why it's so important to tell others about Jesus. Lydia believed in Jesus because Paul was prepared to tell others about Jesus.

Let's pray. Dear God, thank you for the Bible, which prepares us to tell people about you. Help us remember that every season—winter, spring, summer, and fall—is the right time to tell people about you, amen.

This week, every time you use something that helps you prepare for the weather—sunglasses, a coat, or an umbrella, for example—remember to tell about Jesus.

# Paul's Jailer Believes in Jesus

## Bible Story: Acts 16:16-34

> **Bible Verse:** "They replied, 'Believe in the Lord Jesus, and you will be saved' " (Acts 16:31a).

**Simple Supplies:** *You'll need a Bible and rolls of crepe paper.*

You know, some people are put into jail because they tell others about Jesus. The Bible tells about a time when Paul and Silas, two of Jesus' followers, were put into jail for telling others about Jesus. First the people took Paul's and Silas' clothes and beat them up; then they put Paul and Silas in jail. The guards put their feet in chains. Let's pretend that we're chained like Paul and Silas were.

*Help the children pass around the crepe paper. Children should loop the crepe paper around their wrists and then pass it to the next child.*

If you were chained up in jail, what would you do? *Pause for responses.* While they were in jail, Paul and Silas prayed and sang hymns to God, and the other prisoners were listening to them. Paul's and Silas' prayers and songs helped the other prisoners to believe in Jesus. Let's do the same thing. Let's sing "Jesus Loves Me" together. *Lead children in singing "Jesus Loves Me" or another familiar praise song.*

While Paul and Silas were singing, an earthquake suddenly shook open the doors of the jail and made their chains fall away. OK now: Everyone break through your chains, because you are free! *Pause.* If you were in jail and your chains broke, what would you do? *Pause.* I would probably run away from my jail as fast as I could. But that's not what Paul and Silas and the other prisoners did.

The jailer was upset because he thought the prisoners had escaped. But Paul and Silas told the jailer that everyone was still there, that they hadn't run away. After the jailer saw Paul and Silas and all the other prisoners still sitting there the jailer wanted to know what he needed to do to be saved. *Open your Bible to Acts 16:31a, and show the page to the children.* This is what Paul and Silas told the guard: **"Believe in the Lord Jesus, and you will be saved."** Paul and Silas told the jailer all about Jesus. Then the jailer believed in Jesus, and he and his family were baptized.

Paul and Silas said, **"Believe in the Lord Jesus, and you will be saved."** The same is true for you, too. All you have to do is believe in Jesus, and you will be saved. Isn't that great news? Let's pray. Dear God, you are so wonderful! Thank you for showing us how we can be saved. Thank you for loving us enough to save us. In Jesus' name, amen.

*Let the children take a piece of the crepe paper with them as they leave to remind them of the message today.*

SECTION
FOUR

SUMMER
QUARTER

# God Helps Gideon Defeat the Midianites

Bible Story: Judges 6:1-16; 7:1-24

 Bible Verse: "So do not fear, for I am with you; do not be dismayed, for I am your God. I will strengthen you and help you; I will uphold you with my righteous right hand" (Isaiah 41:10).

**Simple Supplies**: *You'll need a Bible and a soccer ball.*

**H**old up the soccer ball so kids can see it. How many of you have ever played soccer? Do you think that if we all teamed up, we could take on the rest of the congregation? All of them? All of them at one time on a really big soccer field?

Well, I think we could—because I've got a plan. *Lean in as if you're calling your team together.* Before we get started, we'd better size up the competition. They're bigger than us. Some of them are probably faster than us. *Toss the ball to someone in the congregation.* Plus, they've got the ball. But I still think we can take them. You agree? Let's give it a try.

*Move toward one side of the worship area, and have children face the congregation.* Here's my plan: First we've got to shrink our team a bit. There are just too many of us. If you have a birthday in a month that starts with a J—January, June, or July—raise your hand. OK, all of you are off the team, but we're going to have you be cheerleaders for our team. *Have the children who are off the team stand to one side.*

Everyone born in a month that starts with an M—March or May—you're now the ushers. You'll help the fans find their seats. *Have these kids join the cheerleaders.*

Who's left? OK. How many of you are left-handed? *If no children are left-handed, ask who was born in the month of February. Keep choosing months until you have one or two children left.* Great! You two [or name of single kid] are on the team. The rest of you will sell hot dogs to the fans at the game. *Have the hot dog "vendors" join the cheerleaders and ushers.*

*Stand with the one or two children who are on the team.* So it'll be just us playing against every single person in the congregation. Do you think we've got a chance against all of those people out there? What do you think of my plan? What do the rest of you think about my plan? *Pause for children to respond, then gather the children together again.*

You know, this is probably how the Israelites felt when they got ready to fight the Midianite army. Here's what happened.

The Israelites had disobeyed God, so for seven years God let the Midianites take control of their land. The Midianites camped in the Israelites' land, ate the Israelites' food, and took whatever they wanted. It was so bad that lots of the Israelites moved to caves way back in the hills.

Finally God told Gideon that it was time for the Israelites to make the Midianites leave. Gideon gathered up an army of thirty-two thousand men, which was just about the right size. Except God said Gideon had too many men. So Gideon let all the ones who were scared go home. Then, when the army went to a stream to get a drink, God said that everyone should be sent home except the men who knelt down and raised water to their lips. Gideon ended up with just three hundred men to take on the huge Midianite army! Even so, Gideon trusted God's plan.

Gideon gave each of his men a trumpet and an empty jar with a torch hidden in it. Then that night his tiny little army snuck around the huge Midianite army. All at one time, they smashed their jars and pulled out their flaming torches. They blew their trumpets. And they shouted as loudly as they could, "For the Lord and for Gideon!"

Let's form a circle to pretend we're surrounding the Midianite army. *Pause for children to form a circle.* Now on the count of three, let's all stomp our feet and shout together, "For the Lord and for Gideon!" We've got to all shout and stomp at once. Ready? One, two, three. *Shout with the children and lead them in stomping their feet. Then have the children sit down.*

The Midianites saw the flaming torches and heard all the noise and thought Gideon had brought a huge army to surround them. They were so surprised and so scared that they all ran away.

Gideon and his tiny army believed what the prophet Isaiah said about God. *Open your Bible to Isaiah 41:10, and show the page to the children.* Isaiah 41:10 says, **"So do not fear, for I am with you; do not be dismayed, for I am your God. I will strengthen you and help you; I will uphold you with my righteous right hand."**

Gideon wasn't afraid because he knew God was with him and his army. We can be brave for the same reason. Let's bow our heads and pray together. Thank you, God, for Gideon's example. Thank you for making us stronger and for helping us when we stand for you. In Jesus' name, amen.

# Samson Receives Strength from God

## Bible Story: Judges 15:9-16; 16:4-30

Bible Verse: "Each one should use whatever gift he has received to serve others, faithfully administering God's grace in its various forms" (1 Peter 4:10).

**Simple Supplies:** *You'll need a Bible and several battery-operated or electric items such as a fan, a flashlight, and a radio.*

Did you know that God can give great strength to people? The Bible tells us that when the Israelites were under the rule of the Philistines, an angel visited a woman. The angel told the woman that she would give birth to a son who would help the Israelites begin to weaken the Philistines' control. When the baby was born, he was named Samson.

God gave Samson a special gift. Let's talk about gifts for just a moment. *Hold up one of the items you brought—the flashlight, for example.* What special thing can this do? Why do we use this? *Pause for children to respond. Then repeat the process with each of the items you brought, and allow the kids to turn the items on and off. As you continue, keep the items on.*

Just as the [flashlight] can [light our way when it's dark] and the [fan] can [keep us cool when it's warm], we can use the special gifts God gives us. These gifts are sort of like talents or skills. Why do you suppose God gives gifts like this to people? *Pause.* Let's see what the Bible tells us about the gifts God gives.

*Open your Bible to 1 Peter 4:10, and show the page to the children.* First Peter 4:10 says, **"Each one should use whatever gift he has received to serve others, faithfully administering God's grace in its various forms."** God gives us special gifts so that we can serve him and others.

God knew it would take a lot of strength to fight the Philistines, so he gave Samson a special gift of strength. Samson used his strength to fight the Philistines, but he didn't always make the best decisions. Because of this, he even lost his strength at one point, and the Philistines caught him. *Turn the power off each item you brought.* What do you think it was like for Samson when he realized he had thrown away the special gift God gave him? What do you think Samson learned from this experience? *Pause for children to respond.*

Remember that our Bible verse says God gives us gifts so we can serve others. Well, Samson asked God to give him strength just one more time. *Turn on the objects again to show their power.* God gave Samson strength, and Samson used his strength to fight the Philistines one more time, and that battle helped the Israelites.

God gave Samson the special gift of strength. What other kinds of gifts do you think God gives? *Help children with examples such as kindness, wisdom, and so on.* How can we use the gifts God gives us to help others? *Turn off the items, and if possible have kids pass one item around. Whoever is holding the item gets to speak and then pass the item to someone else. Again, help children with examples such as "Teaching others about Jesus," "Being kind to others," and so on.* God gives people all kinds of wonderful gifts so we can serve each other. Now I'd like you to turn to a partner and tell your partner one thing you'll do this week to serve someone else. *Give kids a few moments to share. Especially help younger children think of ways to serve others—giving hugs, cleaning up after themselves, or making someone a simple snack, for example.*

Let's pray now and thank God for giving us gifts so we can serve him and others. Dear God, we thank you for blessing us with your special gifts. We're so happy that you allow us to use these gifts to serve you and others. Help us to wisely use your gifts. In Jesus' name, amen.

*As children return to their seats, remind them to follow through on their commitment to serve others this week.*

# Ruth Sticks by Naomi and God

## Bible Story: Ruth 1:1-22

Bible Verse: "A friend loves at all times" (Proverbs 17:17a).

**Simple Supplies:** *You'll need a Bible, a slide projector or unshaded lamp, and a blank wall or projector screen. Before the message, set up a slide projector or unshaded lamp near a blank wall or projector screen in your worship area.*

Let's start our time together today with something fun. *Turn on the projector or lamp, and show children how to make shadows on the wall. Let kids briefly experiment with making shadows, then let each child take a turn in making a shadow individually. Then turn off the light, and have kids sit down.*

Seeing those shadows reminds me of today's Bible story. The story is about two women named Ruth and Naomi. Naomi and her husband had two sons, and they all moved to a place called Moab. Naomi's husband died, and she was left with her two sons. Then the sons got married. Ruth married one of Naomi's sons, but then Ruth's husband died. In fact, both of Naomi's sons died. Naomi was very sad. She told both of the women who had married her sons to go back home to their own families. The one named Orpah did go back to her own family, but Ruth didn't. Ruth told Naomi that she would stay with her because they were friends. Ruth stuck with Naomi, kind of like the way our shadows stuck with us!

*Turn on the light again, and make a shadow for the children.* See how my shadow sticks with me? *Move around so kids can see the shadow moving too.* No matter where I go, my shadow sticks with me.

That's how it is with good friends. No matter what happens, real friends love each other and stick together. Listen to what the Bible says about friends in Proverbs 17:17: **"A friend loves at all times."** *Move the shadow around again.* Friends love each other and stick together all the time just as our shadows stick with us! *Turn off the light.*

Do you have a really good friend? *Pause for kids to respond.* Let's go around the group, and we can each say a good friend's name out loud. I'll start. *Say a friend's name, then let each child say a friend's name.* Let's all try to remember to be the kind of friends the Bible talks about. Let's stick with our friends as Ruth stuck with Naomi. We can ask God to help us. Let's bow our heads.

Dear God, thank you for giving us friends. Help us to love our friends all the time, just as you tell us to do in the Bible. In Jesus' name, amen.

# Ruth Marries Boaz

## Bible Story: Ruth 2-4

> **Bible Verse:** " 'For I know the plans I have for you,' declares the Lord, 'plans to prosper you and not to harm you, plans to give you hope and a future' " (Jeremiah 29:11).

**Simple Supplies:** *You'll need a Bible.*

Hi, everyone. I want to start today by playing a game. *Have the children form groups of three or four.* In your group, you're going to create some shapes together by using your bodies. For example, I'll say, "Make the letter A." Then you'll sit or stand together so you form the shape of a letter A. Are you ready? Make the shape of a tree. *Let kids try to make the shape of a tree for a few seconds.* You guys are really trying hard to make this shape. But you know what? I have a plan for how to make the shape. If you listen to me, you'll be in great shape.

One person could stand straight and tall with hands over head as the tree trunk and upper branches. Everyone else in the group could stand behind that person and hold their arms out the sides as the branches. *Help groups form tree shapes, then applaud the children's work. If you have time, repeat this process with a couple of other shapes—a bike and a flower, for example.*

You guys did a wonderful job following my directions. Was it easier to make the shapes with or without my directions? *Pause for children to respond.* It's often easier to do something when we have plans to follow. Just as I had plans for how to make the shapes, God has plans for your life. Isn't that exciting?

The Bible tells us about the plans God had for a woman named Ruth. Ruth's husband had died, and she lived with her late husband's mother, whose name was Naomi. Ruth and Naomi didn't have very much money or very much food, but they had a plan. Ruth went to work in a field owned by one of Naomi's family members, a man named Boaz. Ruth's plan was simply to gather enough food for herself and Naomi to share. But God had a different plan for Ruth.

*Open your Bible to Jeremiah 29:11, and show the page to the children.* Jeremiah 29:11 says, " **'For I know the plans I have for you,' declares the Lord, 'plans to prosper you and not to harm you, plans to give you hope and a future.' "** God definitely had good plans for Ruth's future. While Ruth was out in the heat picking up scraps of grain, Boaz—the man who owned the field—noticed her. Boaz decided that he liked Ruth, and they got married. Ruth had a plan to keep herself and Naomi from going hungry, but God had an even better plan for making a bigger, happier family!

 Let's think about that Bible verse again: " **'For I know the plans I have for you,' declares the Lord, 'plans to prosper you and not to harm you, plans to give you hope and a future.' "** How does it make you feel to learn that God has plans for you—plans that should give you hope? How do you think we can be sure to live as God plans for us to? *Pause for children to respond.* Because God has good plans for our lives, we can have high hopes. But to make sure we follow God's plans, we need to do what God says is right, and we need to pray and be sure to listen for God's voice.

 Let's say a prayer together now. Dear God, you are truly an awesome God. Thank you for providing hope and plans for the future. Please help us follow your plans for us and do what you want us to do. In Jesus' name, amen.

# God Answers Hannah's Prayer

## Bible Story: 1 Samuel 1:1-28

 **Bible Verse: "Why are you downcast, O my soul? Why so disturbed within me? Put your hope in God, for I will yet praise him, my Savior and my God" (Psalm 42:11).**

**Simple Supplies:** *You'll need a Bible.*

We are going to talk today about a woman named Hannah. Hannah was a very sad woman because she couldn't have a child, and she really wanted one. She was so sad, it felt like she was stuck in a deep, dark hole.

Let's pretend that [name of child] is Hannah, who is so very sad. *Choose one child to pretend to be Hannah. Have "Hannah" sit on the floor, and have the rest of the children stand up behind Hannah. Encourage Hannah to act very sad by frowning, sighing, and pretending to cry.*

Now let's see if we can find a lifeline to help "Hannah." Do you know what a lifeline is? It's something we can use to help someone out of trouble. What can we say to Hannah to help her to feel better? *Have children take turns patting "Hannah" on the back and saying things such as, "It's going to be OK" and "God loves you." Then have the children sit down behind Hannah.*

Thank you for helping Hannah. You know, I think I have just the lifeline to help Hannah. *Hold up your Bible.* The Bible tells us that Hannah used prayer as her lifeline. She prayed and asked God to help her out of her deep, dark hole of sadness. *Firmly hold one end of your Bible, and have Hannah hold the other end. Using the Bible, help Hannah stand up.*

You know, one of the neatest things about Hannah's story is that after she prayed to God, she felt much better. Even though she didn't know how God was going to answer her prayer, she knew that God was in control. That made her feel better. And do you know what happened? God answered Hannah's prayer by giving her a baby. Hannah was so happy, and she thanked God for her baby.

*Open your Bible to Psalm 42:11, and show the page to the children.* In Psalm 42:11, the Bible says, **"Why are you downcast, O my soul? Why so disturbed within me? Put your hope in God, for I will yet praise him, my Savior and my God."** This is exactly what Hannah did when she prayed. She put her hope in God, and she praised him. Because she put her hope in God, she was no longer upset.

Think about a time you felt sad. Think about a time you thought no one would be able to cheer you up. Would anyone like to tell us about a sad time? *Pause for volunteers to respond. You may want to encourage children to share by telling them about a time you were sad.* It's hard to go through sad times, isn't it? We feel the same way Hannah did—as if we were in a deep, dark hole. But God is always with us. And knowing that can help us to feel better, even when we're going through sad times.

Let's pray about this. I'll say a sentence, and then you can repeat after me. Dear God, help us to always praise you. *Pause.* Thank you for always being with us. *Pause.* Help us to remember that you will always help us. *Pause.* Thank you for loving us. In Jesus' name, amen.

# God Speaks to Samuel

### Bible Story: 1 Samuel 3:1-21

 Bible Verse: "Then Samuel said, 'Speak, for your servant is listening' " (1 Samuel 3:10b).

**Simple Supplies:** *You'll need a Bible, three volunteers whose voices may be familiar to children, and a screen or sheet for your volunteers to hide behind. For example, you can hang a sheet from the ceiling or set up a large piece of cardboard near the area where the children will gather. Make sure your volunteers can get behind the screen without being seen by the children. If a screen isn't practical, you can bring a speaker phone to the session or tape record volunteers' voices ahead of time. Let your volunteers know that as soon as children have gathered together, they should get into position.*

How many of you are allowed to answer the telephone at home? *Pause for children to respond.* When you answer the phone, do you always know whose voice is on the other end of the line? *Pause.* Let's play a game to see how good you are at figuring out voices. See if you know whose voice this is. *Have your first volunteer speak to the children from behind the screen.* Whose voice do you think that is? *Let children guess. Then reveal your volunteer's identity.*

Now see if you can guess who this is. *Let your second volunteer speak to the children.* Well, do you know who that was? *Pause as children guess, then reveal your second volunteer's identity.* OK, we have one more to guess. Here we go. *Let your third volunteer speak to the children.* Do you have any idea who that was? *Pause as kids answer, then reveal who your third volunteer was.* Let's give our volunteers a big round of applause for playing that game with us. *Lead kids in clapping as the volunteers depart.*

What was it like to guess who was speaking to you without being able to see the people? Were you absolutely sure who was speaking each time, or did you have some doubts? *Pause for responses.*

The Bible tells us about a time when a boy named Samuel faced a similar situation. Three times, Samuel heard a voice that he didn't recognize just as we heard three voices today. And three times, Samuel guessed incorrectly about who was speaking. But the fourth time, Samuel knew who the speaker was. Do you know who was speaking to Samuel? *Pause.* God was speaking to Samuel! And when Samuel finally realized who was speaking to him, this is what he said.

*Open your Bible to 1 Samuel 3:10b, show the page to the children.* In 1 Samuel 3:10b the Bible tells us, **"Then Samuel said, 'Speak, for your servant is listening.' "** As soon as Samuel realized that God was speaking to him, he was ready and willing to listen to what God had to say. We can be ready and willing to listen to God, too, just as Samuel was. How does God talk to us? *Pause for responses.*

God can talk to us in lots of different ways. God listens when we pray to him, and he speaks to us through the Bible, through his Holy Spirit, and through other Christians. Let's ask God to help us always be ready to listen to him, just as Samuel was.

Dear God, thank you for speaking to us. Please help us to always listen to you. In Jesus' name, amen.

---

# Saul Becomes King

## Bible Story: 1 Samuel 8:1–9:2; 10:17–24

> **Bible Verse:** "He is patient with you, not wanting anyone to perish, but everyone to come to repentance" (2 Peter 3:9b).

**Simple Supplies:** *You'll need a Bible, a marker, small inflated balloons, and one large inflated balloon. Before the message, draw faces on all the balloons. Then hide the large inflated balloon in the area where the children will gather.*

How many of you have things your friends wish they had? Tell us about those things. *Pause for children to respond.* How many of you wish you had things your friends have? Tell us about those things. *Pause.* Parents, have you ever heard the statement, "Johnny has one. Why can't I?" *Allow parents to respond.*

In the Bible, an entire country wanted something other countries had. I'm going to tell you about that, and I'd like you to help me. *Give each child an inflated balloon with a face drawn on it.* You're going to use these balloons as puppets to pretend you're from that country the Bible tells about. Your puppets will be the Israelites in our story. As I tell this story, listen for what the Israelites say. Every time the Israelites say something, use your balloon as a puppet and repeat the words back to me.

God was the leader of the Israelites; God was like their king. Pretty neat, huh? Well, they didn't think so. They began looking around at the other countries and noticed that the other countries had people for kings instead of God. So the Israelites went to a prophet named Samuel and whined, "We want a king." *Remind children to repeat the phrase.* Samuel said, "But God is your king. Hasn't he taken good care of you?" But again the Israelites whined, "Yes, but we want a king like all the other countries have." *Pause for children to repeat.*

God was sad that the Israelites didn't want him to be their king any-more. God told the Israelites that no person would be as good a king as he was. Still, the Israelites pouted and said, "No! We want a king!" *Pause for children to repeat.* So God told Samuel that Israel could have a king.

God led Samuel to a man named Saul. Samuel poured oil on Saul's head—which was a good thing to do in those days—and told Saul that God had chosen him to be the king of Israel.

Samuel called all of the Israelites together and said, "You whined about wanting a king other than God. So God is going to give you what you asked for. God has chosen Saul to be your new king."

The Israelites said, "Where is Saul? Where is our king?" *Pause for children to repeat.*

God told them, "Saul's here, but he's a little shy. Go look for him." *Let the children search the area for the large balloon. When they find it, hold it up for everyone to see.*

Saul was taller than all the other Israelites. When the Israelites saw him, they shouted, "Long live the king!" *Pause for children to repeat.*

 Sometimes we whine when we don't get what we want. But that's not how God wants us to act. *Open your Bible to 2 Peter 3:9b, and show the page to the children.* Second Peter 3:9b says about God, **"He is patient with you, not wanting anyone to perish, but everyone to come to repentance."** Even when we whine and do other wrong things, God is patient with us just as he was with the Israelites. He wants us to realize that what we've done is wrong. He wants us to apologize.

 Let's close our eyes. If you have behaved poorly and are sorry, silently tell God and ask his forgiveness. Dear Lord, God, we are so sorry for our wrong behavior. We want to tell you about those things now. *Pause.* Please forgive us and help us to behave nicely. In Jesus' name, amen.

*Allow children to take their balloons with them.*

---

# Saul Makes a Big Mistake

## Bible Story: 1 Samuel 13:1-14

> **Bible Verse:** "Do not be anxious about anything, but in every-thing, by prayer and petition, with thanksgiving, present your requests to God. And the peace of God, which transcends all understanding, will guard your hearts and your minds in Christ Jesus" (Philippians 4:6-7).

**Simple Supplies:** *You'll need a Bible.*

What are some things you worry about? *Pause for children to answer.*

*Open your Bible to Philippians 4:6-7, and show the page to the children.* In Philippians 4:6-7, the Bible tells us what to do when we're anxious, or worried, about something: **"Do not be anxious about any-thing, but in everything, by prayer and petition, with thanksgiving, present your requests to God. And the peace of God, which tran-scends all understanding, will guard your hearts and your minds in Christ Jesus."** So God doesn't want us to worry. He wants us to pray in-stead. And when we pray about the things that worry us, God will give us peace—even if we don't know what's going to happen.

So what does God want us to do when we're worried? *Pause for children to answer.* That's right. God wants us to pray and ask for help. Then God promises that we'll feel his peace. What do people look like when they're worried? *Encourage kids to show you their best worried looks.* What do people look like when they're peaceful? *Encourage kids to show you what peaceful people look like.*

The Bible tells us about a time when Israel fought another group of people, the Philistines. There were so many Philistines that the Is-raelites were very worried. They didn't think they could win the battle.

Show me again what worried people look like. *Pause for children to show you their worried faces.*

Saul, the king of the Israelites, knew the Israelites needed God's help for this battle. Saul knew that if the Israelites didn't ask for God's help, they would lose the battle. Saul was supposed to wait for the prophet Samuel to ask for God's favor, but Samuel was late. So Saul became very worried. Show me again what worried people look like. *Pause for children to show you their worried faces.*

When the Israelite army saw that Samuel hadn't arrived, they also became worried and started to leave. What did the worried Israelites look like? *Pause for children to show you their worried faces.* When King Saul saw that his army was leaving, he got very, very worried. He was afraid he wouldn't have enough people left to fight the Philistines. Show me what Saul looked like when he was worried. *Pause for children to show you their worried faces.*

So King Saul decided not to wait for Samuel to come even though this was against the rules. When Samuel arrived, he was very angry because Saul had disobeyed God's rule. Samuel told Saul that because he had broken God's rule, God would choose a different person to be king of Israel.

If Saul had prayed to God about his worries, he could have felt God's peace. Instead, Saul continued to worry and then he decided to try to fix things on his own. Acting on his own, knowingly breaking God's rules, was wrong.

What did Saul look like when he was worried? *Pause for children to show you their worried faces.* What would Saul have looked like if he had prayed for God's help with his worries? *Pause for children to show you their peaceful faces.* How would you rather look: worried or peaceful? Which one feels better?

Let's do what the Bible verse says to do: Let's pray about our worries. I'm going to start a prayer, and I'd like you all to silently follow my directions. Let's pray. Dear God, thank you for inviting us to pray about the things that worry us. We want to tell you right now about some things we're worried about. Now silently tell God some things you worry about, such as problems at home or someone picking on you at school. *Pause for children to pray silently.* God, just as the Bible verse said, we want to bring our requests to you. Here are some things we need. Now silently tell God about things you need, such as a new pair of shoes or a good friend. *Pause for children to pray silently.* God, we want to tell you some things that other people need. Now silently tell God about things you know other people need, such as healing for a sickness or a place to live. *Pause for*

*children to pray silently.* Thank you, God, for listening to our prayers and for giving us your peace instead of worries. In Jesus' name, amen.

Now show me one more time what it looks like to feel God's peace.

---

# God Chooses David to Replace Saul

## Bible Story: 1 Samuel 16:1-13

> **Bible Verse:** "The Lord does not look at the things man looks at. Man looks at the outward appearance, but the Lord looks at the heart" (1 Samuel 16:7b).

**Simple Supplies:** *You'll need a Bible and a few pictures of people you know but the children don't know.*

*Show children a picture of someone they don't know, such as one of your relatives or friends.* Look at this picture and describe the person in the picture. *Pause for children to respond. Then show pictures of a few more people the children don't know, and ask them to describe the people.*

Today's Bible story talks about something Samuel learned when he saw some people he didn't know. In the Bible, God told Samuel to find the man God had chosen to be the new king of Israel. Because King Saul had disobeyed God, God had chosen someone else to replace Saul. He told Samuel to go meet a man named Jesse and his sons. One of Jesse's sons would be the next king of Israel.

So Samuel went to meet Jesse and his sons. Show me what people do when they meet someone new. *Encourage children to shake hands with one another, say hi, wave, and so on.* When Samuel met Jesse's son Eliab, he thought, "This must be the next king!"

*Open your Bible to 1 Samuel 16:7b, and show the page to the children.* But 1 Samuel 16:7b tells us that God told Samuel, **"The Lord does not look at the things man looks at. Man looks at the outward appearance, but the Lord looks at the heart."**

So Samuel met more of Jesse's sons. *Again, prompt children to shake hands with one another, say hi, wave, and so on.* But each time, God told Samuel he hadn't chosen that man to be the next king. Finally, Samuel met Jesse's very youngest son. *Again, prompt children to shake hands with one*

*another, say hi, wave, and so on.* Then God told Samuel, "This is the one I've chosen to be the next king." This young man's name was David, and when he was older, he became King David, the great king of Israel!

 Samuel learned an important lesson that day, and it's important for us to learn the same lesson. It's important for us to remember what God told Samuel. This is what God said. **"The Lord does not look at the things man looks at. Man looks at the outward appearance, but the Lord looks at the heart."**

*Show children the pictures again.* God knows so much more about these people than what we know from looking at their pictures. For example, God knows... *Give some specific details about the character of each pictured person.* And God knows even more than that! God knows everything there is to know about each of these people. And he knows each and every thing about *you*!

It's not your outside appearance that's important to God; it's what you have on the inside that counts. What are the kinds of things that we have on our inside that God cares about? *Pause for children to answer.*

 Let's thank God for seeing what's on the inside of people, and let's ask him to help us look at what's on the inside too. Dear God, thank you for looking at what's on the inside of people, not the outside. Help us to see that what's really important is who people are in their hearts. In Jesus' name, amen.

---

# David Defeats Goliath

## Bible Story: I Samuel 17:1-50

> **Bible Verse: "I can do everything through him who gives me strength" (Philippians 4:13).**

**Simple Supplies:** *You'll need a Bible.*

How many of you have strong muscles? Can you flex them for me? *Pause for children to show off their muscles.* Wow! That's a lot of strong people! What is the heaviest thing you've ever lifted? *Pause for children to respond.* And how many of you are good ballplayers? What other things are you able to do? *Pause for responses.* Now how many of you have ever been told, "You're too little. You can't do this." *Pause for children to respond.* And how did being told you're too little make you feel? *Pause for children to respond.*

The Bible tells us about a boy who was told the very same thing. His name was David, the very same David who was Jesse's youngest son. The David whom God chose to be king of Israel when he grew up. Now back in the days when David was still a shepherd, he loved God and worked hard to keep his sheep safe. God gave David the strength to be a good shepherd.

One day David went to visit his three oldest brothers who had joined the Israelite army. When he got there, he saw a huge giant named Goliath who was making fun of the Israelites.

That made David angry, so he said to Goliath, "God's power is with me, and today you will know that God is stronger than you. God is going to let the Israelites beat you today!" And then the most amazing thing happened. David used nothing but stones and a sling, but he won the battle against Goliath. The little man beat the great big giant.

You know, the Bible tells us that God's power is with us, too, just as it was with David. *Open your Bible to Philippians 4:13, and show the page to the children.* Philippians 4:13 says, **"I can do everything through him who gives me strength."**

Let me show you what that means. *Ask for two volunteers. Make sure one of the volunteers is a child you'll be able to lift. Ask the big volunteer to try to lift the child volunteer using just one finger.* Now use just one finger to try to lift [child's name] again, but this time I'll help you. *Lift the child just a little, and quickly return the child to the ground.* That's just what this verse was telling us. Even though we're not strong enough to do some things, God can help us do anything. Isn't that exciting?

Let's close our eyes as I pray. Dear God, thank you for helping us do things that we aren't able to do on our own. Help us to remember to always ask you for your help and strength. In Jesus' name, amen.

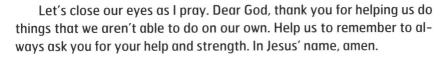

# Jonathan Warns David

## Bible Story: 1 Samuel 18:1-4; 19:1-7; 20:1-42

> **Bible Verse:** "But there is a friend that sticks closer than a brother" (Proverbs 18:24b).

**Simple Supplies:** *You'll need a Bible and masking tape or strips of cloth.*

I want to tell you today about two boys from the Bible: David and his really good friend Jonathan. Do you know who David was? *Pause for the children to respond.* David was a shepherd boy who fought against Goliath and who was chosen by God to be king of Israel. Well, in this story David isn't king yet. But because he fought against Goliath, he spends a lot of time with Saul, the man who is Israel's king. King Saul has a son named Jonathan, and David and Jonathan are best friends. What is it like to have a friend? What kinds of things do you like to do with your friends? How much time do you like to spend with your friends? *Pause for children to respond.* We usually like to spend lots of time with our friends, don't we?

*Open your Bible to Proverbs 18:24b, and show the page to the children.* The Bible even talks about friends. Listen to what it says in Proverbs 18:24b: **"But there is a friend that sticks closer than a brother."** This verse reminds us that some friends are even closer to us than brothers or sisters. Friends share with each other and care for each other and love each other just as brothers and sisters should.

Let's play a game. Everybody grab a partner. I'm going to tape you together to show that you're stuck closer than brothers and sisters. *Tape or tie each pair's wrists together. If you use tape, be sure to leave the sticky side out* so when children take off *the tape, it won't hurt them.*

Now I want you to pretend that you and your partner are stuck together like really close friends. You do every thing and go everywhere together. *Encourage the children to walk around the room, jump up and down, tie their shoes, and so on. After a few minutes, have everyone gather together again.*

David and Jonathan were such good friends that they seemed to be stuck together the way you are. Then one day Jonathan's father, King Saul, became angry with David and decided David should leave forever. David hid while Jonathan begged his father to change his mind. But King Saul didn't change his mind. So Jonathan sent a signal to David, telling David that he needed to leave before King Saul found him. Jonathan and David knew they would probably never see each other again. But remember, because David and Jonathan were such good friends, it was as if they were stuck together the way you all are.

How can you be stuck together with someone even though that person isn't right here with you? How can you be best friends with someone even if you don't see them all the time? *Pause for responses.* We love our friends even when we're not with them, don't we? We're stuck together with someone because that person is always in our hearts and will always be our friend. This is how it was with David and Jonathan. Even though they would never be together again, they knew in their hearts that they would be friends forever!

Pray with me, and let's thank God for the special friends we have. In our prayer, you can talk silently to God about your friends, and then I'll close the prayer. Dear God, thank you for these special friends. *Pause.* Please help us be good friends to others. In Jesus' name, amen.

*Help the children remove the tape before they return to their seats.*

---

# Abigail Makes Peace

## Bible Story: 1 Samuel 25:1-35

> **Bible Verse:** "Do not repay anyone evil for evil. Be careful to do what is right in the eyes of everybody. If it is possible, so far as it depends on you, live at peace with everyone" (Romans 12:17-18).

**Simple Supplies:** *You'll need a Bible and an adult volunteer.*

Today's Bible story is about a very brave woman named Abigail. Often when we think of someone who's very brave, we think of a person with lots of big, strong muscles. Show me your muscles. *Pause as kids respond.* Well, the Bible says Abigail was beautiful and smart. She showed how brave she was without using her muscles. Here's what happened.

Abigail was married to a man named Nabal, and he was kind of mean. David, who God had chosen to become the king of Israel, was camped in the fields nearby. They had been protecting Nabal's shepherds for free. Then David sent his men to ask Nabal to share some of his food with David and his men. But mean Nabal said no, he wouldn't share his food with David and his men. How would you feel if you had done something nice for someone, and then that person was mean to you? *Pause.* David got very mad with Nabal. And he decided to get even. Let's see what getting even means.

*Have kids form pairs, and have partners stand facing each other. Demonstrate with an adult volunteer how to have each partner hold out one hand, palm facing up. Then have partners try to slap each other's hands, without being slapped themselves. Once kids understand how to play, let partners play for a minute or two. Caution kids to slap gently so they won't hurt each other, and watch closely so kids don't get out of hand. Then have kids sit in their pairs.*

In our game, the slaps kept going back and forth. That's how it is when we try to get even with someone—the hurts just keep going back and forth, making the problem worse. The Bible tells us not to try to get even with others. *Open your Bible to Romans 12:17-18, and show the page to the children.* Listen to what the Bible says in Romans 12:17-18: **"Do not repay anyone evil for evil. Be careful to do what is right in the eyes of everybody. If it is possible, so far as it depends on you, live at peace with everyone."**

Now remember, Abigail was the wife of the mean man Nabal. Abigail heard how mad David was with her husband. But Abigail also knew that trying to get even wasn't the right thing to do, and that's exactly what she told David. David listened to Abigail, he understood that she was right, and he didn't do the mean things to Nabal that he had planned to do. Let's see how our game might change, just as David's plans changed because of Abigail's courage in telling him he was wrong.

*Have partners stand facing each other again, but this time have partners shake hands with each other instead of slapping hands.* The Bible says we should live in peace with each other, instead of trying to get even. Let's ask God to help us do that. Let's stand in a circle to pray. *Have kids hold hands in a circle. Pray:* Dear God, help us get along with others, just as Abigail helped David get along with Nabal. Thank you for teaching us how to live to please you. In Jesus' name, amen.

# David Spares Saul's Life

### Bible Story: 1 Samuel 26:5-25

> **Bible Verse: "But I tell you: Love your enemies and pray for those who persecute you" (Matthew 5:44).**

**Simple Supplies:** *You'll need a Bible, construction paper, and pens or pencils.*

What is an enemy? Do any of you have enemies? How do you feel about them? How should you treat your enemies? *Pause for children to respond.*

Let's travel along with David in our story today as we see how David treated one of his enemies. Have any of you ever gone on a bear hunt? *Pause for children to respond.* Well, we're going to "travel" together today. Our story begins with David traveling through the desert. Have you ever been in a desert? What is a desert like? *Pause for children to respond.* Let's crunch through the sand with David. *"Walk" your hands by patting them, one at a time, on your knees in a walking rhythm. As you take each "step," say "crunch." Have kids imitate you.*

As he was traveling through the desert, David learned that King Saul, who had become his enemy, was nearby. He decided to sneak into Saul's camp at night when all were asleep. Have you ever had to sneak somewhere? What was that like? *Pause for responses.* Let's sneak with David. *"Walk" your hands very lightly, and say "shh."*

David found Saul lying on the ground asleep with his spear and his water jug next to him. David's traveling companion wanted to kill Saul, but David wouldn't let him. Instead, David took Saul's spear and water jug and left the camp. Let's walk with the spear and water jug. They're heavy, so we'll have to walk slowly. *"Walk" your hands slowly. As you take each "step," say "ugh," as if you're carrying something very heavy.*

David climbed to a hill above the camp. Have you ever gone climbing? What was that like? Let's climb with David. *Move your hands as if you're using them to climb up a hill.* When he got to the top of the hill, David yelled down to one of the guards that the guard had not protected Saul very well, because David could have killed him when he snuck into the camp. Let's yell with David. *Hold your hands around your mouth as if you're yelling.*

Saul heard what David was saying and thanked David for not killing him. He told David that he wouldn't try to hurt him anymore. David told Saul to send one of his men over to get his spear. Let's walk over to get the spear. *Pat your knees in a walking rhythm, then hold out one hand as if you're receiving something.* So Saul and David went on their ways. Let's clap our hands for such a happy ending. *Clap hands in applause.*

How did David treat his enemy in this story? What do you think you would have done if you were David? What would you have done if you were Saul? *Pause for responses.* Let's read a Scripture that tells us how we should treat our enemies. *Open the Bible to Matthew 5:44, and show the page to children.* Matthew 5:44 says, **"But I tell you: Love your enemies and pray for those who persecute you."**

Wow! The Bible says we should not only love our enemies, but also pray for them. Why do you think it's important to pray for your enemies? Do you think you can love your enemies and pray for them? *Pause for responses.* It isn't easy, but we can follow David's example.

To remind you to love and pray for your enemies, I'd like you to use this construction paper to create a symbol of love. Just tear a shape out of the paper that reminds you of what it means to love and pray for everyone, including your enemies. For example, you could make the shape of a heart for love, a hand for helping, or a cross for prayer. *Give kids each a sheet of construction paper, and give them a few moments to tear out their shapes. Then ask volunteers to share what they made.*

Your symbol can remind you of the way David treated Saul. Now, on one side of your symbol, I'd like you to write or draw one way you will try to show God's love to your enemies this week.

 *Give each person a pen or pencil, and give kids a few moments to write or draw.* Let's pray for our enemies now. I'll start the prayer, and then I'll pause. When I pause, I'd like you to finish the sentence, either out loud or silently, with the idea you wrote on your symbol. Dear God, thank you for showing me the right way to treat my enemies. Please bless my enemies and help me to show them God's ways by... *Allow kids to fill in the sentence by praying aloud or silently.* In Jesus' name, amen.

Take your symbol with you, and put it someplace where you'll see it often. Every time you see it, I'd like you to take a moment to pray for your enemies.

# Scripture Index

# How are you driving home families' faith?

What if families could talk about the same Bible story they just studied on the way home from church? What if children could be involved in worship that's just for them? What if kids could build meaningful relationships that brought them closer to God? What if pastors could fuel all that family togetherness by connecting worship with Sunday school, children's church, and midweek? Now they can. Now families can grow in their faith together throughout the week, both at church and at home. Now they can grow spiritually like never before, because FaithWeaver™ brings the entire family together. On the same road.

Encourage everyone in your church family to grow spiritually—together. With FaithWeaver, everyone in your church studies the same Bible story on the same day. At Sunday school. During children's church or in a children's sermon. Even during midweek programs. Which means your entire church family grows—together!

FaithWeaver Bible Curriculum Student Books, Teacher Guides, and Resource Packs help you cover the significant Bible stories you want students to know and trust for ages infant through Grade 6. You'll find most of the preparation already done for you, so you can spend time building relationships with your kids! And included in each Resource Pack you get an easy-to-use CD loaded with stories, sound effects, dramas, memory-verse songs, and more to help drive home your lessons! Leader Guides are also available for **FaithWeaver™ Youth Bible Studies** and **FaithWeaver™ Adult Bible Studies.**

So bring FaithWeaver™ to your church, and see everyone from the nursery to the adult classes grow in Christian faith—together.

# Welcome to FW Friends! A revolutionary approach to children's programs.

Get your elementary and preschool kids excited about their Christian faith with FW Friends™! It's the only midweek program that draws kids closer to God by building stronger relationships—with God, their peers, and mentoring adults—through the power of small groups. You can use FW Friends as a midweek program or for Sunday school, an after-school program, or anywhere you want kids to grow closer to God. Everything in FW Friends is designed to help kids know, love and follow Jesus.

Everything about FW Friends emphasizes lasting spiritual growth. After gathering with their families for a meal, kids go to the Opening Celebration, separate to join their Circle of Friends as they rotate through Discovery Centers, take time for quiet reflection with their journals, then rejoin the other groups for the Closing Celebration.

FW Friends is easy and flexible. Every lesson and activity is clearly and visually laid out in several handy See-It Do-It™ leader guides. Any leader can actually sit down with a group of kids—See-It Do-It guide in hand—and lead them through any activity...with very little preparation needed!

FW stands for FaithWeaver™ and FW Friends is part of the FaithWeaver family of Christian growth resources. Contact us for more information about this family of resources that ties together Bible curriculum, children's church, midweek programming, and the home. FaithWeaver builds on the power of the family to encourage Christian growth.

# Fun Lessons for Children's Ministry!

## Children's Church Specials

Here are 15 new, easy-to-lead worship sessions—each built around a specific characteristic of God! Children will learn to know and love God as they participate in upbeat praise, a memory-building activity, and worshipful prayer. As an added benefit, six of the worship services connect to holidays. This is a must have for every children's church!

ISBN 0-7644-2063-1

## Bold Bible Kids

Encourage your kids with these 12 character-building lessons, each based on a different child in the Bible. Children will discover how God has used little kids in *huge* ways and continues to use kids today! Includes historical information that helps kids connect with Bible characters, and suggestions for encouraging positive, godly character traits in the lives of children.

ISBN 0-7644-2114-X

## Helping Children Live Like Jesus

Introduce your children to Jesus with these 13 lessons...and do it in a way your children will remember forever. Here's active learning at its best—with crafts, skits, art projects, interactive stories, object lessons, and guided group discussions. Your children will examine the life of Jesus from birth to his resurrection—and along the way fall in love with him.

ISBN 1-55945-681-7

## Ready-to-Do Children's Message Kit

It's all here in one colorful package—everything you need to get kids listening...learning...and wanting to come back for more! There are fun gizmos plus step-by-step directions in an easy-to-use book packed with 24 children's messages. You'll deliver unforgettable, active-learning messages. And you'll appreciate how all the preparation is already done for you!

ISBN 0-7644-2029-1

Order today from your local Christian bookstore, order online at www.grouppublishing.com, or write: Group Publishing, P.O. Box 485, Loveland, CO 80539.